SPIRITUALITY
TO GO

Also by Olive M. Fleming Drane

FAMILY FORTUNES: FAITH-FULL CARING FOR
  TODAY'S FAMILIES *(with John Drane)*

CLOWNS, STORYTELLERS, DISCIPLES

SPIRITUALITY TO GO

RITUALS
AND
REFLECTIONS
FOR
EVERYDAY
LIVING

Olive M. Fleming Drane

DARTON·LONGMAN+TODD

First published in 2005 by
Darton, Longman and Todd Ltd
1 Spencer Court
140–142 Wandsworth High Street
London SW18 4JJ

ISBN 0 232 52663 X

A catalogue record for this book is available from the British Library.

Designed by Sandie Boccacci
Phototypeset in 11/14pt Times New Roman by
Intype Libra Ltd
Printed and bound in Great Britain by
Page Bros, Norwich, Norfolk

Alethea

Mark & Laura

Andrew & Fiona

To all those who
nurture my
Spiritual Journey

John

Ruth & Daniel

CONTENTS

Writing this book has been an interesting learning experience for me. Just when I thought I was getting to the end of it, new possibilities kept presenting themselves as I listened to the questions and concerns, and heard the stories, of other people. Just one example: I live in a farmhouse in the middle of nowhere, and unless I am going off on a journey it never really occurs to me to lock the doors. But recently, staying at my daughter's apartment in a large city I became aware again of the importance of security, as the last thing we did each time we went out was to set her burglar alarm. I began wondering how we could invest with spiritual significance such an everyday action as punching the numbers into the alarm. It occurred to me that doing this with intention would allow us to focus on the purpose of our journey, trust our spiritual source for direction and strength, live with integrity, and invite the divine to inhabit the mundane – thereby reconnecting what seems to be ordinary with what is sacred. In other words, reframing traditional spiritual disciplines to meet our present needs.

Many of the rituals and reflections gathered here have developed over the years as I have worked at creating a spiritual space in my own life that would nurture my children, me and my husband. This book began with my awareness that I was doing this, and was motivated by wondering if I might be unique, or even peculiar, in this respect. I have been fortunate to have made trips to far-flung places all around the world, and as I shared the concept with people in different cultural contexts I repeatedly found myself enriched by others who were eager to share their personal spiritual pathways with me. Many of them relished the opportunity to tell me of their own rituals, while others would claim they had none – and then would come back to me later and say, 'When I thought about it, I realize I do have rituals: I just never thought about them in that way.' Another significant source of inspiration has been a small group of international people who met once a week in the chaplaincy centre at the University of Aberdeen throughout the autumn of 2003, taking a different topic each week and sharing the rituals we already practised while exploring new possibilities together.

I owe special thanks to a number of people, not least to Virginia Hearn, my editor at Darton, Longman and Todd, who shared some of her own reflections and rituals with me. I also have to thank my husband John, whose willingness to experiment with the themes presented here has made a significant contribution to the final shape of the book.

I hope that, as you read, this book will become a serviceable tool, helping you explore new opportunities to encounter the divine in everyday life, and enabling you to multiply these experiences as you share them with your networks of family and friends. For those who wish to follow this through on a regular basis, visit my website where I share these and other ideas for infusing daily life with spiritual meaning: www.spirituality2go.com.

OLIVE M. FLEMING DRANE
October 2005

CHAPTER ONE

Rituals
and
Reflections

*Just as a candle cannot burn without
fire, so people cannot live without a
spiritual life.*

Siddhartha Gautama, the historical Buddha (c.563–483 BC)

*A life is either all spiritual or not
spiritual at all. No one can serve two
masters. Your life is shaped by the end
you live for. You are made in the image
of what you desire.*

Thomas Merton, American Christian monk (1915–68)

1: The Rituals of Life

There has been a remarkable revolution in recent years, and the
rituals of spirituality – with or without an overt connection to
particular faith traditions – are an increasingly common part of
everyday life in western societies. When Princess Diana died
in a Paris car crash on 31 August 1997, political and social
commentators who had long since relegated any sort of spiritual

expression to the history books were taken aback by the overt public expressions of grief. A central element of that was the spontaneous creation of shrines in public spaces through which people expressed their deepest feelings. This has been a growing trend in British culture over the last twenty years or so, beginning with public responses to the sinking of the ferry *Spirit of Free Enterprise* off Zeebrugge in 1983, followed by the spontaneous spiritual outpouring of anguish after the death of many Liverpool football supporters at the Hillsborough stadium in 1989, not to mention many lesser and more local expressions of a similar kind.[1] It is now a commonplace sight to come across flowers and other icons fastened to fences by the roadside, marking the spot where someone has died – and also challenging us all to drive carefully.

There is a temptation to dismiss this as mere sentimentality. Long before the emergence of such public rituals, the anthropologist Mary Douglas characterized a person interested in rituals as 'one who performs external gestures without inner commitment to the ideas being expressed.'[2] But the same could be said of many activities we engage in, which lose their true meaning once they are reduced to formality that is devoid of any serious significance. In his book *The Meaning of Ritual*, Leonel Mitchell proposes that the question for us today is not whether we need rituals, but how and when we will use them.[3] Though the term 'ritual' tends to invoke religious images, there are many ordinary things that might be described as rituals: blowing out candles on a birthday cake, shaking hands, exchanging gifts and kissing under mistletoe at Christmas, or receiving a certificate at a graduation ceremony. Robert Fulghum has traced the way we use rituals to mark everyday events quite literally from the cradle to the grave.[4] Such activities need not necessarily carry spiritual meaning, but they can, and probably do more often than we realize.

So how is it that one person lights a candle and it is just a pretty light with which to decorate the dining table, while for another the lighting of an identical candle expresses a much deeper reality which can readily be identified as a ritual, and indeed may well be regarded as a significant expression of spiritual intention? Throughout Western society there is a growing awareness of a need to identify new ways in which our rationalized lives can be endued with a sense of purpose and meaning. Life has become increasingly stressful for many: those who are in work find that it seems to occupy more of their time than was the case in previous generations, and 'leisure time' is frequently more of the same, with the constant demands of domestic paperwork and (in Britain at any rate) our obsession with do-it-yourself projects to remodel our homes. In an attempt to become more efficient, we have compartmentalized our lives. Those with no work find that though they may have a lot of time on their hands, it is not difficult to fill it with meaningless activity. There is a discernible yearning among many people to reconnect the various parts of our lives in such a way that we can experience a sense of personal interior harmony that will also spill over into our relationships with those among whom we live, work and spend our leisure time. Politicians and business leaders, as well as 'ordinary' people, talk about the need for a work/life balance, while life coaches (a non-existent profession until relatively recently) seek to empower their clients to achieve a holistic lifestyle which will combine the detoxification of body, mind and soul with the search for inner peace and wisdom.

It is not difficult to uncover some of the reasons for this growing sense of discontinuity and fragmentation. For a hundred years and more, we have been encouraged to adopt a very mechanistic approach to life, believing that everything operates in a world of cause and effect and that science and technology would not only resolve our problems, but would also improve the human race and in the process make the world a better place. This meant emphasizing and valuing reason over above intuition, a way of being which has eventually left us spiritually dehydrated at the start of the twenty-first century. Descartes' famous phrase, *cogito ergo sum* ('I think therefore I am') became the benchmark for our understanding of what it means to be most truly human, and rationality was elevated above everything else. We are indeed rational beings – but that is not the whole story. We also have emotions, feelings, and relationships. We are not isolated individuals but are intrinsically connected to one another, and in turn to the entire cosmos. Our more distant fore-bears had no sense of discontinuity. When a medieval farmer sowed seeds and tended the crops, these operations were every bit as spiritual as being at prayer: a successful harvest depended not on technology, but on the divine power behind the elements of the natural world. Moreover, work itself was most likely to be a community activity, with support and advice generously given by those who were interdependent on one another.

Today, the nature of work is different. We no longer live in self-sustaining communities and our choices are increasingly limited by global decisions, with the result that the flow of work, and of war, prescribe the possibilities for most people. All these factors distance us from the natural networks of support that sustained previous generations – and so many Westerners find themselves searching out a therapist who will help them to access the wisdom that former generations would have found at their grandmother's knees, or which would have been passed on to them in story form through a shared oral tradition. Growing numbers of people are feeling disenchanted, trapped in a spiritual cul-de-sac – not wishing to abandon the benefits of science and technology (clean water, antibiotics, electricity, and so on), but desperately desiring a way to nurture those parts of our being that we cannot see and, in many cases, cannot articulate. Tom Driver makes a connection between our anxiety-ridden culture, the loss of ritual, and our possible futures: 'To lose ritual is to lose the way. It is a condition not only painful but also dangerous. Some people it destroys. As for the whole society, sooner or later it will find rituals again, but they may be of an oppressive rather than a liberating kind. Rituals have much to do with our fate.'[5]

So where can we find wisdom to guide our lives at the beginning of the third millennium? Previous generations turned to their inherited religious traditions as the obvious source of spiritual nourishment. Today, though, many people regard formal religion as being, at best, out of touch with their daily life experience – and, at worst, as hierarchical and manipulative. Formal religious worship tends to take place in particular times and places, rather than being available as a 24/7 spirituality to match our 24/7 lifestyles. In a world of many conflicting voices, we have become aware of the need for each of us to take responsibility for our own spiritual welfare, and the development of personal ritual is emerging as a significant way of doing this. It has the capacity to connect us with our innermost realities, in the process reminding us of our place in the universe and our relationships with other people as well as with our own bodies. For ritual is primarily an embodied spirituality, which is why in this book we begin with our everyday experiences, and seek ways to explore all dimensions of life by celebrating the ordinary and then unpacking the experience in order to discern the spiritual. In the words of John Lundquist, 'Ritual is the primary means that makes communication possible between humans and the powers beyond immediate human life – the transcendent. Ritual is the process through which contact with the world of the numinous powers is activated.'[6]

Let me give you two contrasting examples. I asked a woman who regularly goes to church, 'When you go into church, what do you do?' 'First I find a seat', she replied, 'then I sit down, close my eyes, bow my head and count slowly to forty.' 'Why do you count to forty?' I asked. Her response: 'Well, that seems to be about the length of time most people do it for.' Conversations with others revealed that many churchgoers do this – but instead of counting to forty, they pray. The fact that this habit was intended to be a space for spiritual encounter had never occurred to this person, even though she was in the place where one might expect spiritual things to happen.

By way of contrast, I have been living in California for the last few months. One of my goals during this time was to learn in-line skating. Given my ability at sports, it was not a foregone conclusion that this was in any way achievable. However, I have mastered it – not with great style, but with a confidence that means I stay upright and blend in among all the fine-looking people in this part of the world. I suddenly realized as I skated along the beach path at Santa Barbara one day that I was looking out across the most beautiful blue water through waving palm trees, and my legs were moving in a regular rhythm – while in my head and in time with my movements were echoing the words of a mantra I have often used in meditation: 'Jesus Christ, God's Son, my Saviour' (derived from the acronym of the letters in the ancient Greek word for fish, which was an early Christian symbol – *ichthus: Iesous Christos Theou Huios Soter*). The action became a prayer: I was taking exercise, having fun, and reaffirming my faith – and doing all three at once! Having mastered the art of skating like this, I was practising at Santa Monica beach one morning, and as I stopped for a rest I got into conversation with a retired man. On learning that I was visiting from Scotland and teaching about spirituality in a theological seminary, he became quite animated and told me how he frequently went to the redwood forests or the desert to explore his own spirituality. He had grown up with a religious background but commented that 'such a rational way of being was good for writing a shopping list but not for the business of daily living'. I think he was in a process of discovering the reality of a spirituality for everyday life, and spurred me on to reflect on Leonel Mitchell's observation that 'One function of ritual in the present world is to give a sense of identity and community to those who would otherwise have none.'[7]

As you explore some of my suggestions for 'things to do' here, you can either use them alongside the life events I mention, or tailor them to your own needs. There is no 'right' or 'wrong' way: mix and match until you find what works for you. We are all individuals, and something that might be profoundly moving for one person will leave another completely cold. So don't be afraid to try out something new or use a suggested ritual in a different way. By being intentional in the desire to explore the spiritual, we discover new insights and wisdom as we unpack the experience. In the process we can expect to connect not only with that other part of ourselves that we label 'spiritual', but also with the transcendent reality which is to be found at the heart of all things, and with which our ancestors were so much more in touch than we in the West typically are today (and, of course, from which people of other cultures have not always been so isolated).

Here's one to start you off right away. Freeze alternate layers of red wine and water in a container (you'll find they freeze separately), then when it is completely solid take it out onto a dish that will be deep enough to hold it all. It will start to melt, but will take quite a time to dissolve. Perhaps do this with a group of friends who are exploring spirituality together. To begin with, this solid block is cold, rigid, lifeless, and its riches not readily accessible – a bit like institutional religion appears to many folk today. But as time passes, this water and wine will melt, the mixture will become life-giving, meaningful, and useful. You can drink it, and enjoy its refreshing properties. Water and wine were the ancient symbols of God's relationship with people, the divine and the human mixed up together. We are not intrinsically dry in ourselves, but the presence of God enriches our being. A group of us did this, and because I was in a hurry, I had placed some already frozen raspberries in the middle of the wine to speed up the process of freezing. I have to admit that I also cheated a little and speeded up the melting process by softening the block in the microwave oven before bringing it to the table. It stood in the centre of the table while we shared food – moving, living, dissolving as we watched. By the time we finished eating and moved onto the coffee, we were ready to share our observations. The most surprising came from Hilary, a twenty-something American woman, who suggested, 'Let's try it in our coffee.' Most of us thought this was a crazy idea, but after much laughter one person (an African from Malawi) tried it and pronounced it to be good, so one after another we all followed his example. We were amazed not only by the taste but also by the conversation, as we connected this somewhat offbeat experience with other things that were going on in our lives at that time – the colour, the ingredients, the taste, and more besides. We never got round to franchising the blend! But we did agree that it gave us all a new angle on an old saying, found in the Bible at Psalm 34:8, where the poet encourages us to 'Taste and see that the Lord is good; happy are those who take refuge in him.'

2: Living in the Moment

With today's pressurised lifestyles, few of us get the opportunity to take a big view. We have to live from day to day. Though we are committed to bigger visions, the immediate moment is what grabs our attention, and along with the sense of fear that pervades many people's minds there is a growing awareness that the present is the only time we can be sure of. It is now more important than ever that we know how to redeem each moment by living with an intentional connection to our ultimate spiritual purpose.

The following chapters suggest numerous ways of doing that in the context of everyday life. Some of these rituals are explained later, but others feature regularly and will be worth describing here in the rest of this chapter. Possible uses of them will be explored in later chapters. But remember that there is no 'one size fits all' for life rituals, and we all need to discover for ourselves meaningful ways of expressing our own spiritual concerns. My preferences are not intended to be prescriptive, so be creative: mix and match, have fun as you experiment – then share your own discoveries with others.

Every child is an artist. The problem is how to remain an artist when we grow up.

Pablo Picasso, Spanish artist (1881–1973)

Candles

It is easy enough to light one: strike a match and ignite the wick. But in exploring the spiritual, you need to be intentional, investing your actions with meaning. Choose a candle with care, giving thought to size, colour, whether to have it scented or decorated, and if so how. While completing this book I held a weekly session exploring this topic with a group of university students. Each session began with the lighting of a tall four-inch thick golden church candle, as we took a moment of quietness to centre ourselves. The same candle regularly sits on my kitchen table, where some of the same students gathered on Sunday evenings for dinner to unpack their experiences, share stories and encourage one another. After about four months, one of them commented, 'That candle is everywhere I go!' Its light had become part of him, while others had barely seen it. So how can the same action be significant to one person and unnoticed by others? In exploring our spiritual side, intentionality is central as that raises our awareness of many things, and we begin to see the sacred in the ordinary as the culturally imposed boundaries between sacred and secular are dissolved.

Be as diligent about extinguishing candles as you are in lighting them. I have seen people light candles as a symbol of hope, only to have them subsequently blown out. Safety requires us to extinguish candles eventually, but empathy requires we do not extinguish the spiritual encounter by doing it while someone is still exploring their journey. In a group setting, I would always extinguish the candle only when everyone else has left the room. The use of tea lights can get around this, as they have a limited life and burn out naturally.

Keeping a Journal

Choosing a book is the first thing. If you enjoy writing, then a lined book and a pen which gives you pleasure to hold will be part of the intentionality in your choice. Keep it in a special but handy place. If you are likely to write while in transit – in the bus or train while commuting, for instance – or in a spare moment, then choose a journal that is easily transportable. It can still be attractive (I have a small square one, spiral bound with a multi-coloured plastic cover). If you intend to collect bits and pieces of other things – a ticket, a flower, a sequin, a programme, what-ever – then always have something you can store them in, such as a small purse or an envelope that can contain them safely until you get home to work on your journal. By definition, a journal should be filled in regularly – not necessarily every day, but if there is too long an interval between entries your enthusiasm, and memories of what you want to record, will fade. It is for your own personal use, so needs to be tidy enough to satisfy only yourself. But the care you invest will be an indication of how serious you are about this, and that can be a learning experience in itself. Providing yourself with a special book will put value on your work and give it more significance. Being special need not equate to cost, though, and the cheapest scrap-book can be decorated to become as distinctive as one crafted from the finest handmade papers.

Keeping a journal can bring healing into the lives not only of those who write them, but of their readers as well. For an example of that, read Nicholas Wolterstorff's book *Lament for a Son* in which he writes about the death of his son. From my mail-bag, I know that my own book, *Clowns, Storytellers, Disciples* has fulfilled a similar role for many who read it – and again, while it is not a journal in the narrow sense, it records my own story in a way that connects with others.[8] In all this, think laterally in relation to your own skills: a video diary is a journal by another name.

GRAPHS

A graph is a journal in another visual form. Make a simple graph by drawing a line horizontally across a piece of paper and then dividing the line into sections, each of which can represent any time frame you choose – the last week, month, year, your entire life. The time frame will determine how many marks you need. You can then plot above and below the line the highs and lows of the month, week or years. Join the marks up, and see what your graph looks like. You may decide to do this with someone you trust, in which case you can each share your graphs and talk through them. This is a helpful way of enabling someone else to talk through a problem. For instance, a child who says 'I don't like school' may be helped by plotting the week's happenings and discovering which things were good and which were not. Even if it all appears bad, the very act of drawing it on paper may facilitate talking about it in a way that would not happen if they were bombarded with ambiguous questions, like 'Whatever is wrong with you?' You will then be in a better position to help.

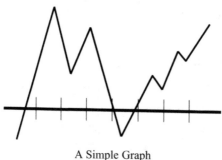

A Simple Graph

COLLAGE

By a collage, I mean a collection of things attached onto a large sheet of paper or card – usually by glue, though this is not the only way it can be done. You will need a suitably sized card, something for attaching other materials to it, and a good space to work at. Your collage could be something you create for a single significant event, or you may make a series. In the latter case, you will want to keep them like a portfolio.

When making a collage, experiment and don't be inhibited. You can add absolutely any materials, from ribbons to dried pulses such as lentils or barley, sequins, name tags, literally anything that will stick. The choice is limited only by your imagination. Words will take on a new form if cut from papers or magazines – in different sizes and scripts and also by adding hand-drawn letters in distinctive colours or paints. You might even explore the use of calligraphy as a result of this. If a special phrase really impacts you, then work on this and frame it. Whatever you do, don't just fill up a blank piece of paper. Choose a symbol that says something about you. Perhaps draw an outline of yourself, or the shape of your house, car, or favourite toy or ornament, and then fill the space with significant items in as simple or as intricate a way as you wish. I recall one of my students at Fuller Seminary making a whole life collage, shaped like himself and about two feet square, which had such a profound impact on him that he laminated and displayed it in a prominent place even after he graduated.

THE SIGNATURE BOOK

Get a book with a good quality paper that opens flat, and a pen with a real nib that uses ink from a bottle. So choose a distinctive pen, and an attractive bottle, perhaps using several colours. Fold a page in half to make a crease down the middle, and then open it again. Write your signature along the fold, then while the ink is still wet fold the dry half of the page over the writing and press and smooth it down. If you have used enough ink, a mirror image is transferred and the result can look quite exquisite. You might want to try this on rough paper before doing it in an actual book. In some places I have suggested using this with a group, to mark a special occasion, in which case you could collect the signatures on separate sheets and then bind them into a folder. That will avoid disappointment if someone makes a mess or is unhappy with their result. It is also worth getting people to write or print their signature with a normal pen in the corner of the sheet, so you know who is who. The smallest child can be included – this is the way they make butterfly pictures in nursery. It could be more personal still by including thumbprints, while some artistic folk may wish to embellish the result.

As I write this, I think of Sarah. She did a presentation for me yesterday in a class with which I had previously shared this ritual. She told of how she grew up feeling ugly, stupid and of no worth, simply because that was what she repeatedly heard as a child. She then asked the class 'Why does a painting like Van Gogh's *Irises* attract thousands of visitors?' 'It's because of the little signature in the corner,' she said. She went on to draw our attention to the following words she had come across when she was in school:

> When I look at your heavens, the work of your fingers, the moon and the stars that you have established; what are human beings that you are mindful of them, mortals that you care for them? Yet you have made them a little lower than God, and crowned them with glory and honour. You have given them dominion over the works of your hands; you have put all things under their feet, all sheep and oxen and also the beasts of the field, the birds of the air, and the fish of the sea, whatever passes along the paths of the seas. O Lord our Sovereign, how majestic is your name in all the earth![9]

Then she commented, 'I discovered I *am* special; not because of how I look or if I have a high IQ but because I am made in the image of God. I have God's signature on me. That's what makes me special.' She concluded by signing to a song and as we listened and watched we could all see that signature quite clearly. But it was the book in which she placed her own signature that created space for that transformation.

Meditation

It is easy in today's busy world to be rushing around attempting to accomplish everything to meet deadlines and in the end be like a cat chasing its tail. We've all done it, convincing ourselves that we have no time when actually if we took time and reflected we could short-circuit some of the hassle. Meditation requires a space that will facilitate the process. Some people can only find this quietness indoors – others will take time to go into the countryside or seaside, and those with the time and cash may go to a spa or on retreat. One mother I heard of with several small children used to put her apron over her head! When they saw her do that, the kids knew not to interrupt.

However you choose to do it, the principle is the same. It is about taking time out from everything else and being physically still in order to be inwardly still. Breathe rhythmically and become conscious of the physical movement of the body and the sound of the breath alone. If other noises interrupt, just acknowledge them and let them go. Don't dwell on them. For some, repeating a single word or a phrase will facilitate the stillness which is the prelude to meditation. Many people adopt terms chosen from sacred scriptures, but you can also use such things as a photo, a stone, or other object, and meditate on them. Time taken out to do this will energize our own spirits as well as creating a space in which we might encounter the divine Spirit whose presence we so often miss because in our 'normal' busy state we exclude or close down our spiritual vision.

The unexamined life is not worth living.
                    Socrates, Greek philosopher (469–399 BC)

CHAPTER TWO

Beginnings and Endings

1: The start of all things

Pregnancy

We will not all become parents, but most of us will at some time be close to those who are. Every pregnancy is unique, though the expectation of a first child always heralds the greatest number of changes. Life will simply never be the same again, and new parents have a lot of adjustments to make, psychologically as well as physically.

Intentional rituals are particularly helpful in times of change, and creating something appropriate can be a great way of helping expectant parents enjoy that nine months of preparation and adjustment to their new roles.

- Build in a special time each week to reflect on the changes that pregnancy brings, choosing particular music to share with the unborn child – something that can bring calmness to the pregnant woman as well as contributing to the baby's well-being.
- Copy those images of ultrasound scans and share them with grandparents and other relatives or friends (and older children, if you have them) to initiate what will hopefully be long-lasting bonds between them and your child.

the birth of this child, and you are responsible for his or her ongoing nurture. To accomplish that effectively, you will need to be in touch with your own spiritual side, and for most of us the use of simple daily rituals is a good place to start exploring that. You can begin soon after the birth, by recording in a special card your feelings of the moment, and storing it in your newly-created box of memories. Do it there and then rather than waiting until later: you probably won't get the time, and you will miss the immediacy of this special moment.

Baby Comes Home

New babies often have to occupy a space that was previously used for something else, which means that other stuff has to be moved out. This process can itself become part of the rituals of preparation. Just as you have prepared for the birth by looking after the mother and unborn child, get the room ready to receive this new arrival. Even mundane things like painting and decorating can play their part in a spiritual preparation for the birth.

If you are well organized, you will be doing this before the birth, and talking to your child as the work proceeds: describing what is happening, how the colours look, and playing relevant music as you work, can all be part of the preparations. This is also a very practical way to include the father-to-be as well as other older siblings. As you all feel the baby growing and kicking this is also a good time to reconnect with the reality of prayer. Pregnancy and birth gives us an intuitive connection to deeper cosmic processes, and at this time it seems more natural to talk with the Creator in much the same way as you might talk to your best friend.

Beautiful things need not be expensive. I bought a very simple basket for my first son to occupy during the first few months of his life, and when my subsequent three children arrived the scrubbing and redecoration of this wicker cradle itself became a family ritual. The crib has now been passed on to my oldest son and the same process became a ritual in his family.

When my first children were born, I was not well off and could never afford to buy all the fancy things that were in the shops. I made small sheets by cutting up larger sheets which had worn out in places, but still had enough sound fabric in them. Cutting them, washing, and then stitching hems around their edges brought me as much delight as going out and buying far more expensive items, and all that became a ritual of preparation in itself, an offering of myself and my talents to the one I was expecting.

When baby enters his or her new room for the first time, do something grand and ceremonious. Play the music you have been enjoying during pregnancy. Bless the space with a prayer or some other reflective action. Healthcare professionals and other visitors are bound to arrive, but don't let that inhibit you. You will never be able to recreate or repeat this special moment, though if you make it special you will always remember it and recount it to your child. Once you have a routine, you will find regular activities such as washing and dressing your baby can easily be infused with spiritual meaning. Touch is one of the most significant spiritual connections you can make with another person – and you will be touching your baby a lot in these early days. Why not integrate your everyday caring for a young baby by intentionally blessing your child on a regular basis? If you feel comfortable doing so, you could use baby oil to make the sign of the cross (or some other symbol which has significance for you).

Unexpected Complications

Pregnancies do not always go smoothly, and advances in medical technology have made some things even more complicated. In past generations, for example, the loss of an embryo or a twin in early pregnancy would have gone undetected, whereas today it is not only detected but also reported, which itself creates multiple uncertainties for expectant parents, who naturally worry about the survival and health of the remaining embryo. Even after birth, there can still be unexpected health issues. It is especially important to be aware of the situation for yourself, as very few people seem to know how to empathize with parents at such times. Even good people can seem aloof and disconnected, often because they have no idea what to say, and do not want to create more pain by being intrusive. Wise folk know that at such times words are less important than tears and touch.

A prayer for times of uncertainty

God who promises to bring light into dark places
Turning pain into opportunities of
        transformation
Come and pierce our darkness now
Give us the courage to face the future
Be our strength.

Sometimes, parents find themselves with no baby to bring home. Coping with this is probably the hardest thing most of us will ever encounter in the whole of life. We naturally want some rational explanation, and that can lead to unnecessary anguish over guilt, because the most obvious thing to ask is, 'who was to blame for this?' or 'what could I have done differently that might have prevented it?' Even close friends tend to be lost for words, and have no idea at all about how to be part of the sorrowful experience, which means that most people in this situation are left to struggle with it on their own. The unexpected nature of such tragedies underlines the importance of having established life rituals as a way of accessing and celebrating spirituality in everyday situations. Those who have an underlying pattern of this sort will have a resource that, while it may not answer any of the questions, will provide strength to survive. I know, because I have been in a very similar situation to the one I am describing, and it was established rituals of daily living that – among other things – helped me most in the darkest hours. Prior to the loss of my daughter, I had been in the habit of praying with my small son as a regular everyday ritual, and that just continued. Indeed, on more than one occasion he initiated such prayer in the insistent way that only a five-year-old would – though to call it 'prayer' may well create the wrong sort of image, as it was more in the form of desperate conversation with hard questions addressed to God. His childlike trust at that time made a significant contribution to my personal recovery, which probably goes a long way towards explaining why I have come to regard nurturing the spirituality of our children as a high priority.

A prayer in time of crisis

We are devastated.
We did not know emotional pain could be this
   intense.
Our expectations never envisioned the present
   reality.
Time is standing still.
If only there was somewhere to run to.
But no one can put the clock back.
Things will never be the same again.
People tip toe around us as if walking on egg
   shells.
Our hopes lie shattered like shards of glass.
Tread carefully among the splinters,
Rescue the fragile pieces,
Join them together to create a new shape
And in your mercy illumine them,
For without your help we will sit in darkness and
   without hope.

Adoption

In one important sense, an adopted child is doubly special because you have specifically chosen him or her. The fact that no pregnancy preceded the child's arrival might also mean you have more time and energy available for things like preparing the space. Much of what has been written above will still apply – things like playing beautiful music and meditating or praying for your new child while decorating their room. Depending on the child's age, or any special needs that might need to be taken into account, there will be particular things you will want to include. If your child is no longer a baby, you will not want to bring them into a perfectly finished environment as it will be more fun to do much of the arranging and choosing together, depending on their age and skills. You can start your book or box of precious things in advance of the child's arrival by including items depicting your own history, along with pictures of the process of your preparation. If the child is a baby, their story will to a large extent become your story. But for an older child bringing his or her own story to this new relationship, the process will be slightly different and working together on making a box of memories could itself be a ritual that will create a space within which child and adoptive parents can reflect on their own distinctive identities at the same time as a new shared relationship is in the process of creation.

There are only two bequests we can hope to give our children. One is roots; the other, wings.

Holding Carter

2: Rites of Passage

Stages of life were traditionally celebrated through the marking of rites of passage. They still are in most parts of the world, though there are only a few residual ones left in Western culture today. Children are now exposed at a young age to adult attitudes on topics such as sex, and when this is combined with the growing pressures of study and the need to succeed from a young age, it is not surprising that the nature and extent of childhood is changing radically. Children now have to assume responsibilities that in the past would not have come to them before reaching maturity, and that is blurring the distinctions between those stages of life that the inherited rites of passage were designed to mark. But it is still worth making the effort to mark some transition points so that the growth of our young people is endued with some kind of significance.

Naming and Baptism

Giving a name to an unborn child helps to identify them, even if it is only a term such as 'the bump'. Choosing a name can be difficult, because it is the one thing your child cannot easily escape from in later life – though by giving more than one, we can at least provide some choice to the child in later life. Virtually all cultures mark the birth of a child in a celebration involving the wider community of family and friends. Traditionally, this has focused on a religious ceremony, though in some countries (including the UK) it is now possible to have a non-religious naming ceremony through the offices of the same state-appointed registrars who keep records of births and deaths. Many people celebrate a child's birth more informally in the home. Whatever the context, it is good to include gifts of thanksgiving, along with poems, paintings, a piece of music, maybe a dance, or whatever else might be a relevant expression of joy and thanksgiving. A collage can be a good thing to create on such an occasion. Everyone present at the thanksgiving event can make a contribution, or a memento of the occasion can be created more simply by mounting in a book the messages of congratulation that were received, or keeping them in a specially decorated box.

Older siblings should always be prominent in a thanks-giving event, maybe lighting a candle for the new baby, while you could also initiate a simple game along the lines of 'I wish/pray for lots of happiness for Susan'; or 'I pray for wisdom for Andrew'; 'I wish for long life for Fraser'. You could indicate in the invitations that this will happen, so that folk can think about it and maybe bring a tiny symbol which will represent their wish or prayer. Prepare and line a basket to receive the symbols, and have a book ready so people can write their request for the child and sign their name alongside it. Then add some photos of the event before putting it all in a safe place for future reference.

Now for a couple of fascinating examples of how per-sonal rituals can be incorporated into regular church liturgies (both of them took place in the Church of England). At one traditional baptism in church, everyone was given a square of fabric as they arrived, on which they wrote their wishes for the child. Then the two grandmothers stitched the squares together to form a cape which was placed around the baby, who was then quite literally clothed with the prayers and good wishes of family and friends as she was baptized.

Another way of physically expressing solidarity with a new baby and his family began with small bottles of spring water, sourced from a company that invests its profits into water purification programmes in the developing world.[1] Everyone present got one, along with a pen and a luggage label on which to write or draw their aspirations and prayers for the child. The labels were tied onto the bottles, and each person took a sip of water as a sign of their ongoing support, before pouring the remaining water from their bottles into the font to become the water of baptism.

Another fascinating ritual was shared with me by a Native American from the Navajo tribe, where the first person to see a baby smile throws a party in celebration.

First Steps

My first child walked unaided on his first birthday, his brother did so at thirteen months – something I remember not because it was a month later but because for the previous two weeks he had been 'trapped' in various restricted spaces during a very wet camping holiday. On being lifted from the car on my return, he stood up and ran the full length of the entrance hall of the house. Such incidents mark important passages in our lives, and imprint themselves in our shared memory. If we have a camera to hand and are quick enough to capture the moment, we are doubly fortunate. But in any case, mark the occasion in a journal or by a photograph taken soon after. Remember, though, that these are not the only first steps. We all take many 'first steps' both as children and adults, and the confidence and balance with which we take these steps will be critically influenced by the support we receive. Sometimes a spoken comment will be enough, accompanied by a smile, and maybe a token gift, a card, or a symbol linked to the event or activity. Because you will know the folk who are taking the new steps, you should experiment with ideas of your own to find something particularly significant. It could be a simple thing, like a shell from the local seashore offered to someone embarking on a long journey.

First Words

Some first words are spoken so distinctly that it's easy to catch them, like my second son who first said 'sheep'. In other cases it is only after some weeks or months that we realize that what sounded like babbling was actually words. You could capture the word(s) in cross-stitch, or by framing something that represents the first speech – not the actual word 'dadda' (or whatever), but maybe a photo of the item or person, with the peculiar pronunciation written underneath. One word I particularly remember from one of my children is 'boobibary' ('library' – it was a man who painted the house who clarified its meaning for me by pointing out that it was a hybrid created from 'books' and 'library').

Like first steps, there are also many 'first words': a presentation to the class in school, a job interview, an oral exam, the first day at work. All deserve a token from someone to mark the occasion and make it special. Offering encouragement after such first words is also important. If it has been a grand speech then it is comparatively easy to give praise. If there have been some difficulties, this is not the time to point them out, but to be encouraging and look for ways to facilitate and nurture for the future. It is, however, important to find a way of having integrity so that what you say is believable. If someone really made a mess of things, they will already know that themselves and will not be helped by being told that it was wonderful. Better to put the occasion in perspective and show them how they can build on the experience, and then continue to be encouraging and supportive when it comes to the 'second' and subsequent sets of words.

New School

This is both a beginning and an ending, and whether it is primary school or graduate school it brings closure to the past and new possibilities for the future. Going to school for the very first time can provide a child the opportunity to break with a habit that has been carried on from babyhood and which is becoming embarrassing – like taking a favourite blanket everywhere. In the place of a comfort blanket, why not create a special bag that contains some small but distinctive and personal items that can give a sense of security in the new environment? In transitioning through middle or senior school, frame a photograph of achievement at sports or some other skill, and make a gift of some piece of sports equipment or other practical item that will be useful, but not so desirable that it will be too attractive to thieves. At some point in a child's development, a personal mobile phone will indicate a certain level of maturity as well as providing a non-embarrassing way for parents to keep in touch, especially if they use the text messaging facility rather than making voice calls. Progressing to having a regular allowance for clothing items and personal effects will help to develop a sense of responsibility towards money.

Transitions through schooling always evoke a mixture of excitement and apprehension. Help a child to be well prepared by telling them how you felt yourself, and that way they will understand that their feelings are not unusual, nor are they the only one to experience them. Helping them to talk about it will enable them to work out some of their fear. Give a special pen, or notebook, or bag, or some other useful thing – perhaps something so small that they can feel it in their pocket without anyone else even knowing. That will give the reassurance that someone cares.

I have always made a specific point of praying with my own children, holding hands at the same time and letting them know that I will continue to pray while they are going through the experience. You may be surprised how easily such simple rituals grow with them to become valuable tools for life. While writing this book, I got a phone call from my daughter late one night. Now a medical student, and reflecting on exams that were coming up, she asked me, 'What is that verse about not relying on your own cleverness?' Fortunately I recalled it right away: 'Trust in the Lord with all your heart, and do not rely on your own insight. In all your ways acknowledge him and he will make straight your paths.'[2] I followed it up by email the next day with another verse I remembered subsequently: 'If any of you is lacking in wisdom, ask God, who gives to all generously and ungrudgingly, and it will be given you. But ask in faith.'[3] I was encouraged that, facing a new situation, the memory of what had been done when she was a child reminded my daughter that God is alongside us at every stage of life.

University and Further Education

Parents have different ideas of how to give financial support to their student children. Some send a weekly or monthly allowance, though my preference has always been to start off by giving an allowance that should last for the entire first term away from home. This has the advantage of giving a young person the responsibility of managing their money over a longer period of time, but without the sense of abandonment. If it goes well, that is fine. If (as is probably inevitable) mistakes are made, then next term will bring a new opportunity to start over again. If your young people adapt well in the first year, and if you can afford it, then why not give them what they will need for a full year or more: that way, they have even more scope for longer-term financial planning, and they can also get the benefit of the interest paid while the cash is in their own bank account. Have an agreement that no matter what happens, they will not borrow money without discussing it with the wider family first. A loan might well be the most sensible thing, but make sure it is only taken out after discussion, and have a clear understanding of who will eventually pay for it.

The end of any course of study gives a major opportunity for some kind of ritual, and all institutions have their own leaving traditions that can often be quite elaborate, especially in colleges that have been around for centuries. There is never any shortage of photographers wanting to offer graduation pictures. For a more personal touch, why not create a signature book among friends?[4] No matter what the level of achievement, always have any certificate framed and hung up with pride – and do what it takes to get your young people to attend their graduations or presentations in person. But do it for their sake, not for yours – and especially not because you have funded them and want to get your money's worth. Consider a gift specific to their future work, such as a pen for a lawyer, scissors for a hairdresser, and have it personalized with an engraving.

First Date and First Break-up

Dating should be in the standard school curriculum. It always has been in America, though in Britain the emphasis tends to be more on sex education than on social skills (how to participate without becoming pregnant or diseased). This is one of those instances where many parents only appreciate the contribution they could have made when it is too late to do much about it. But if nurture has been intrinsic within the family from the start, then proposing some realistic ground rules, helping to choose something special to wear, and using one of the rituals the young person has come to treasure – perhaps combined with a gift of perfume or aftershave lotion – will go a long way to help.

Not many people spend the rest of their lives with their first love, so it is almost inevitable that teenagers and young adults are going to move in and out of different friendships. One secret is not to get too heavily in a relationship when either person knows there is no chance of long term commitment: there will be less to undo, and less pain, as a result. The reason this occurs in the first place is often down to poor communication. Parents and others can help by providing opportunities for young people to get to know each other well in the presence of many different people. It is important for those concerned to know what the expectations are on both sides, and if one or other is having second thoughts a lot of anxiety can be avoided by saying so at an early stage. It is important to be both gentle but honest, treating others in the way we would wish to be treated ourselves. If the break-up is a mutual decision, it may be possible to stay friends, though that will be harder if one is profoundly hurt in some way. A parting gift or symbol may be appropriate to mark a changing relationship – maybe a CD, though probably a new one rather than one containing music that has connections with previous special occasions, which may be too painful at this stage. Parents should always encourage their teens to talk and listen to their friends before the parting, so they can understand each other's feelings for the future. Whatever parents do, breaking up with a boy or girlfriend for the first time can seem like the end of the world. Adults know that time will heal, but that doesn't seem so obvious at age fifteen or sixteen. The hurting teenager will need support, but may not want that to be obvious, so parents need to read this well. *Knowing* your child helps, of course. Even so, two kids in the same family might react quite differently. A ritual diversion may help, maybe going out and doing something special, or perhaps doing something special at home, like cooking favourite food or watching a film together.

Engaged to Be Married

The framework within which we now form relationships is changing all the time. I am sticking here with the traditional pattern of engagement followed by marriage not because I am unaware of the popularity of more informal living arrangements, but because this is making it easier to write the book, and also because other forms of cohabitation are basically variations on this same theme, and therefore similar rituals can also be appropriate even though the legal framework might be different. For all these reasons, to decide on marriage is an even bigger step of public commitment than it used to be in past generations, and young people who do this are now the exception rather than the rule. So make it really special for them. A particularly worthwhile gift could be a place on one of the various courses that aim to equip people for this stage of their lives. Every young person I have known who has gone on such a weekend has come back singing its praises as a most worthwhile way to prepare for some of the challenges of married life, including matters such as earning and spending money as well as more intimate aspects of life in relationship.

The Eve of a Wedding

It is always worth the effort of bringing the two families and their close friends together for some formal meeting in advance of a wedding. The night before is often a good time, especially if people have to travel some distance just to be there. To meet for the first time on the day of the wedding is bound to be tricky, and certainly will not be conducive to getting to know people in any significant way. But keep an eve of wedding event simple, as the next day will be hectic enough – though do include some food and drink, as this enables everyone to relax. It's also an opportunity for recruiting other helpers: people always feel more included if they have a specific role.

For a ritual, get two people – one from each family (one male, one female) – and write some reflections and aspirations which are specific to the given family. Here is an example I have used on such an occasion:

We give thanks for
    bringing A and B together,
    the love they have for each other,
    their skills which have brought them
        employment,
    their voluntary contribution in their
        community,
    their health and strength and ability in
        sport.
We pray for success
    in their chosen career paths
    their aspirations for their life together.
Help them to
    respect each other at all times
    be quick to acknowledge their mistakes and
        apologize

find in each other's family true community
nurture one another by their care and
   concern
to create a truly spiritual place they can
   call home.
Let tomorrow be a day of joyous celebration,
   a day of new beginnings.

This will become a truly significant event if you personalize the statements to the young couple and their families. Depending on the time of year and the climate where you live, you might invite everyone to light a candle and make a silent wish/prayer for the couple. Then place the candles in a designated place. For a summer wedding it's nice to do this outside at dusk, while at other times of the year or in a cool climate a special ambience can be created by clearing away dishes from the table, playing some soft music and subduing the lighting. Whatever you do, take care to provide a safe place for lighted candles. Recognize, too, that different people will feel comfortable in different ways: some might want to sit on the floor and create an informal atmosphere, while others prefer chairs. Wait till everyone is settled before reading the reflections so that all can join in the responses from the beginning. Remember to give the couple a copy of the words you used, mounted in a presentation card. They will appreciate this in days to come because the next 24 hours are going to be so busy that they will not catch all the detail. You might well find that going back over the aspirations in this card will become for them part of their own anniversary ritual and enable them to reflect on their journey, and whether in the days ahead they want to make adjustments.

Wedding

Creating meaningful rituals for a wedding can be both daunting and fun. Many weddings in secular settings can seem cold and clinical, while religious weddings in church can appear archaic and out of touch with life. There is no need for it to be like this. There is no reason why every wedding should be the same and, though the legal requirements vary in different jurisdictions, there will invariably be more scope for diversity within the marriage service than most people realize. I have taken part in such events in different religious traditions and different countries, and have been surprised at the excitement of couples when they discover that things are not as fixed and unchangeable as they imagined. There is something very special about a couple choosing rituals that have integrity with who they are. It can be of particular value to include close friends and family as participants (rather than spectators) – and why not also give some careful thought to the words you want to say, so that the promises made match your intentions?

Here are some creative ideas to include in a wedding. Some are ancient traditions, while others are of more recent origin. From my own personal experience, I can say with confidence that all of them are entirely practical within the context of any sort of marriage ceremony.

- At a traditional Jewish wedding, a wine glass is wrapped in cloth and then stamped on by the couple, symbolizing their transition to a new family.
- Invite the mothers of bride and groom to compose prayers of thanksgiving and request for the couple, and then to read these at an appropriate point in the ceremony.
- Invite a close friend or family member to officiate.
- Have significant people such as those who baptized the couple participate in the service.
- The wedding celebrant(s) can go to meet the bride as she enters the church, rather than her being 'given away' in a

traditional way (something that many couples are not altogether happy with nowadays).

- The couple themselves can say a psalm or piece of poetry together.
- Siblings of the two families perform readings or play music.
- Create your own personalized invitations and stationery, rather than having them printed by a commercial organization.
- Create your own order of service or ceremony, in partnership with your celebrant for the occasion. There will always be some legal requirements to be incorporated, but these need not be particularly limiting. In Scotland and much of the USA, for example (as distinct from England), the only requirement is that a couple state their intention to take one another in marriage, but the actual words in which that promise is made is very much a matter of individual choice.
- Introduce a 'blessing of the rings' with a difference. Slot the rings onto a long ribbon, which can either be tied to form a circle or passed out along the rows of seating in a church or other venue so that everyone has a section of ribbon they can hold. The ribbon can be colour coordinated with the clothes worn by the wedding party, and you could also pleat two ribbons together to symbolize the joining of two families, maybe with two differently coloured ribbons representing something distinctive to each family. The celebrant takes the rings and starts them on their journey along the ribbons, and as they are passed to each person in turn this is an opportunity for everyone present to bless them and to express their wish for the couple, articulated either out loud or silently (e.g. 'I pray for harmony for Bruce and Tracey', 'I ask for long life ...' and so on). After everyone has taken part, the rings are untied from the ribbon and exchanged. If guests are notified in advance about this, they have longer to consider what they will say. And if there will be too many guests for everyone to do this at the wedding ceremony itself, it might be appropriate to have this as part of the eve of wedding

ceremony, in which case the wedding rings are brought to the ceremony already blessed.

- An old tradition recommends that the bride wears 'something old, something new, something borrowed, something blue'. This can be invested with rich meaning perhaps with the passing on of a treasured piece of jewellery from a grandparent or other relative. If there is not the legacy of something old this might be the time to give something new that can be treasured in the future, or even to lend the item. The important thing is not so much the value of what is passed on, but the act of doing so, which in itself acknowledges the family heritage, along with the support being offered to this new commitment, and expectations for the future.

- At one of our family weddings, which was to be attended by people of different faith commitments, instead of the conventional Christian blessing at the end of the grace that started the meal, everyone present let off a party popper, which not only matched the mood of celebration but also made prayer more accessible to those with no prior experience of any kind of spiritual dimension to life.

- There is something special about both giving and receiving a banner that greets a couple as they come for their wedding ceremony. Create one from fabrics that connect with significant items such as the bride's and bridesmaids' dresses, the men's waistcoats, or significant ethnic designs such as Scottish, Spanish, Mexican, or whatever is relevant. For the big day itself, trimmings of fresh flowers can be used, but remember that the couple will wish to keep such a banner, so make it of a size that can conveniently be hung in their home.

- Make small bags from scraps of the wedding fabrics and fill them with lavender or potpourri to be treasured as mementoes of the occasion. It may be possible to make special ones for close relatives and simpler ones for others.

- Create a special signature book just for this one day.[5]

- Place disposable cameras on each table at the wedding meal, to give the guests the opportunity to catch some informal moments that would otherwise be missed by official photographers.

Divorce/Separation

Traditionally, love and marriage have gone together. For many couples, it is now marriage and divorce. No matter how openly we deal with this, divorce is always going to be a difficult time, and it is inevitable that there will be some degree of hurt and resentment. Some kind of ritual of closure will almost always help, and the importance of this is now being recognized by faith communities around the world, some of whom have well developed resources for use in such situations.[6] In circumstances where both parties accept the fact that their best way forward is separation or divorce, they may wish to create a ritual together. In this case, choose some symbol of your shared life, including a mixture of those that affirm both bitterness and sweetness. Acknowledge the aspirations and dreams that have floundered, and where possible admit to one another the responsibility that each has brought to the situation. Give to each other the gift of forgiveness, perhaps exchanging a flower or token that symbolically releases you both to a new phase of life. Having a third party facilitate this will generally be helpful, as that can create a safe space within which failures can be acknowledged, while ensuring that no one individual accepts inappropriate blame. For a couple who made their original vows in church, it may bring a greater degree of completion to acknowledge before God their feelings of failure and exasperation (or whatever), asking forgiveness for the past, healing for the present and grace to move forward into a new future.

This is not fantasy, but is rooted in my own experience of helping people in actual life situations. Some people are indeed able to separate in agreeable and harmonious ways, and with appropriate support many more could reach this level of mutual self-understanding. But for others, all this will be too idyllic to be true. Where a mutual ritual is not possible, or in the case that only one partner wishes to participate, then different ways of marking the end of a relationship may be helpful. Again, having the help of supportive friends or a spiritual adviser will always make a difference. You could gather together significant items – photographs, or other symbols representing the relationship in its various stages – and work through the same emotions as expressed before. Acknowledge the loss of dreams and hopes and your own part in the failure, without taking on inappropriate blame, especially if you have been the victim of physical or mental abuse. Ask for help to bestow forgiveness on your partner and grace to enable you to move forward. It may be helpful to write your feelings on paper and shred or burn these sheets as a way of letting them go and marking the end. Or you could choose stones, casting them into the sea or a deep river, or fallen leaves which can be scattered to the wind in an open space, saying some personally chosen words as you do so.

One thing that is unlikely to be helpful is the destruction of things like wedding rings, marriage certificates, or photographs. These are all part of your personal story, and can be treasured for that, even though you may wish to transform them in some way. For example, wedding rings could be sold and the proceeds used for some specific work of goodness, which in itself is an affirmation of the possibility of new opportunities and transformation. Or they could be turned into jewellery for your children. The inclusion of children in any ritual of separation needs careful thought, and to some extent the conclusion you reach will depend on their age and personal development. It is probably a good idea to talk this through with a therapist or spiritual counsellor along with the children. But generally speaking, all members of a family are likely to be better equipped to cope with the ending of such a significant stage of life if they also are included in the ritual.

Remarriage

The circumstances of remarriage are diverse. For some, it comes after the death of a former partner, whereas for others it follows divorce. Either way, the relationships are always going to be more complex a second time around, if only because you are connected to more networks of people at this time. Past memories may conflict with the new start, and issues from the past that appear to have been laid to rest can surface unexpectedly. Being intentional about seeking help from a good counsellor will help here (just as it will in the context of a first marriage). Those who move from one relationship to another without addressing the factors that led to the failure of previous marriages will face the possibility that the new relationship might fail for all the same reasons as before. This is one reason why the rituals of separation and divorce can be so important. But of course, the celebration of a second or subsequent marriage can be just as joyous and empowering as a first marriage – and all the ways of enhancing the experience described above under weddings will also be relevant here.

3: Changes and Transitions

Starting and Finishing Work

Work is characterized by many beginnings and endings. We begin and end our work every day, and in that context a daily ritual can be used as a commitment to doing a good job at the start of the day, and reflecting on how it has gone at the end. One of my friends has a daily prayer sent to his computer, and the first thing he does when he switches it on is to collect that from his email inbox, and use it to give a focus to the day's work. Connecting with the outside world in this way also keeps us in touch with wider realities than just our own lives.

In terms of starting work on a longer time scale – a new job – then mark it by buying something particular to help yourself at work, perhaps with your name engraved, such as a pen or tool set. If it is a career change then mark the end of one era and the start of another in one of the many ways suggested in chapter 4 for regular events. These points of recognition prevent us from accumulating untidy ends which leave us confused. It could be as simple as a final drink with our colleagues and shredding old files and notes.

Eventually, we all come to the end of our working life. The very thought of retiring from work fills many people with horror. There is nothing surprising about this, as Western culture has taught us to define our essential identity by reference to the work we do. It is worthwhile – and natural – to have a celebration with colleagues to mark the completion of your working life. But it is also important to consider in advance what you will do on retiring. Work out a plan to continue eating healthily, taking exercise, giving time to friends and building new friendships, as well as pursuing interests that there has previously been insufficient time for. Include the possibility of exploring totally new things. Consider cultivating some options which you will be able to pursue even if you are not always as fit and flexible as you are now. This might all sound like commonsense, but it is surprising how many people miss what is obvious. We can find new opportunities through serving others. In the UK, one such organization to explore is Christian Vocations which operates an extensive programme of opportunities for those over 50 who can spare anything from one hour a week to a couple of years, and with various financial options covering everything from those who have retired on a good pension and need no further income, to those who can give their time but require their expenses to be paid, and also including those who would need to have full-time remuneration.[7] You can search the worldwide web for more information about other organizations – and if you don't know how to do this, then join a class to learn. That in itself can open up new horizons. Maybe if you have never kept a journal now is the time to start, perhaps writing your own story to gift to your grandchildren.

Menarche/Menopause

This is perhaps more important today than in previous generations, as the onset of menarche often occurs when a girl is quite
young. This is a time to articulate the fact that as a woman she is
'made in the image of God' (Genesis 1:26–27), and to talk
around what that means in everyday terms. A ritual here might be
to have an anointing, a sealing of hope, with words like '[the
name] you are a woman made in the image of God: be all that
you can be, all that God intended'. Give some perfume or oil so
she can anoint herself each month and remind herself of her
unique importance to God. Likewise, at the opposite end of the
childbearing years, it is just as important to realize that a
menopausal woman is also 'made in the image of God' and to
have an anointing and prayer at this time. This kind of blessing
could be helpful to include in a group, where those who already
know each other well through prayer or some other regular
communal activity can feel free to share such intimate knowledge with one another. Men and boys can be a little more
diffident about this kind of thing, but to have a similar ritual for
them with similar timing might enable them also to understand
what it means to be a man 'made in the image of God'. To have
an anointing for men that was monthly might help them to be
more open about their bodies, allowing them to be more in touch
with their feminine side and appreciating their own connection to
the natural world. In relational terms, it encourages them to be
less macho and hierarchical, and appreciate a sense of mutuality
between the sexes.

Growing Old

*Be not afraid of growing slowly: be
afraid only of standing still.*

Chinese proverb

We can all now expect to live longer than our forebears, and even old age is no longer what it once was: you can be deemed old enough to retire at fifty, but have another forty years of life to look forward to after that! Large numbers of older people enjoy an independent and worthwhile old age. My father-in-law is in his nineties, lives alone, and works with 'older people', all of whom are younger than he is! But when independent living is not an option, that can create other issues that can helpfully be addressed through rituals that connect even these struggles with the deeper meaning of all things.

When parents go to live with their own adult children, previous roles are reversed: the children are now the carers and providers, and the fact that those being cared for are older than the care-giver creates its own challenges. Preparing a space will be the first challenge. You will want to give your parent(s) a degree of choice in the changes that will be made, but right from the start it will be necessary to establish some ground rules to prevent one generation being overbearing towards another. This sounds good on paper, but in terms of how it works out a lot will depend on the temperament of those involved. Recognize that you will need regular time out from one another. Particular pressure is generated if structural changes to your home are necessary, which may not be your preference. So encourage the parents to put their own stamp on their personal space, but ensure that the rest of the house remains in your style. Above all nurture your sense of humour. Make moving-in day special by inviting particular friends of your parents, thereby creating a ritual to mark the occasion. Depending on what they feel happy with, you could orchestrate a blessing of their room (but don't impose your preferences, and remember that an older generation might not feel as much at ease with the concern for spiritual meaning that is part of today's lifestyles). Recognize that your children (their grandchildren) might be in a better position than you when it comes to organizing a meaningful celebration. Plan for some favourite music, poetry, or prayers. Give a visitors book for this new stage of life (maybe one designed and decorated by your children), and all those present on the first day can sign it. Maybe include a gift of a coffee machine, or some other item that will help to give a degree of independence. Whatever you do, it is always going to be worth doing something, rather than opting out because it seems too big a challenge. Although grandparents and grandchildren often connect with each other more easily than parents and children, the typical teen does love loud music, and this can easily lead to friction between the generations. You could turn the potential discord into a preparation ritual by sound-proofing either the space that the older relative will occupy, or (perhaps to everyone's benefit) the teenager's bed-room. It could save you hours of family squabbles afterwards, while the teenagers will appreciate the freedom to be themselves without interruption.

For older people to move into residential care is a big step for them, but also for their family. Here again, some carefully chosen rituals may help the transition. It is important for the one moving into care to have as much involvement as possible in the decision-making process, rather than being presented with a done deal, even if this is in their own best interests. Most people in this situation have misgivings, and worry about getting it right, and what might happen if they don't. There are going to be fears on both sides, so be kind to yourselves. It is easy to keep good contact in the early days, but as time passes good intentions can be overridden by the conflicting demands of everyday life. Mark the moving with an exchange of significant token gifts, and then think of little ways to keep the contact going that will be manageable within the context of a busy lifestyle. There are many ideas throughout this book which could be adapted to these different circumstances and it is worth using rituals that people have found helpful in the past, even if it means developing them in a slightly different way, giving continuity with their past. There is however no substitute for human contact. For those who are part of a wider group or faith community, members of the group can be encouraged to give additional visits. Some people are just naturally gifted at relating to older people, and in a society with an aging population we will need all the help we can get from such individuals. Professional care staff have increasing opportunities to provide rituals that will be relevant to their clients, as government agencies are realizing the importance of spiritual care in this context (and in some places this is now a statutory obligation). It is important to develop things that not only connect with the residents' past experience but will also be participatory rather than simply doing things for them. There is an increasing awareness that ageing offers a time for spiritual development, even when the body is becoming weaker. There is significant work to be done with older people in the community and in residential care if we are to develop holistic living throughout life.

Happy are those who find wisdom,
and those who get understanding ...
She is more precious than jewels,
and nothing you desire can compare with her.
... Long life is in her right hand;
in her left hand are riches and honour.
... She is a tree of life to those who lay hold of her;
those who hold her fast are called happy.

Proverbs 3:13, 15–16, 18

4: THE FINAL JOURNEY

In Western culture, death is one of the few points at which we still expect things to be highly ritualized. What is appropriate will vary enormously, depending on the circumstances: the age of the deceased, whether or not the death was expected, and so on. Professionals can sometimes give the impression that what happens at a funeral is totally non-negotiable, and as a consequence people find themselves living with regrets that they were not able to have the sort of service or committal that they really wanted. Professionals do this for the best possible reasons, recognizing that it is a traumatic moment and not everyone wants to be burdened with the detail of such things. But if you are one of those for whom the detail matters, then don't allow what look like the normal conventions – or the expectations of others – to divert you from your inclinations. Include the things that are important to you and the person who has died. In particular, think carefully before excluding children. Though it might seem wise to shelter them from the reality of death, it can have the opposite effect by leaving them ill-equipped to deal with it at all. Death invites us to look beyond the grave and to acknowledge that life and death are part of the same journey – something that children intuitively know to be true, even if they lack the conceptual framework within which to express it. I remember at the grave-side of my mother-in-law, it was my six-year-old son who stood next to his grandfather and was able to slip his hand into the older man's hand, saying by his action what nobody else knew how to articulate. Later on, as a teenager, he took the bold step of asking if he might play his flute at the funeral of a family friend (a man in his early sixties). As his mother, I was nervous for him, thinking he may be asking too much of himself, but his concern was directed to acknowledging his friendship with the person who had died, and supporting those who had been bereaved.

A child's funeral is always particularly difficult, but the hope of resurrection was summed up for me in the experience of a friend who conducted the funeral service for a two-year-old boy. While the child had been ill and confined to bed, his mother had put crumbs on the windowsill of his room and every day a robin came to eat them, much to the delight of the family. At the graveside, as words of Scripture were read and prayers were said, a little robin came and sat by the coffin. This was in the middle of summer in England, a time of year when for some reason robins are not often seen. Then the bird flew away. The child's mother and my friend caught each other's eye for a moment in a look of recognition and reassurance that the child's spiritual journey was continuing. Such events cannot, of course, be planned, but those who are in touch with the spiritual side of their nature can perhaps expect the Creator to send such intimations of immortality for those who wish to see them.

As I have researched this book, some of the most lovely rituals I have been given have concerned death.

- At the funeral of a young father who died tragically, a book was created for everyone to sign and include their address 'so that in days to come, the children would know the great number of people who had respected their father'.
- An elderly lady had for many years carefully kept a visitors' book for her friends to sign, whether they were calling for a coffee or an overnight stay. At her funeral, those who came to celebrate her life were invited to sign their names from the back forwards bringing a sense of thanksgiving and completion to her life.
- A newly ordained priest, eager to be truly relevant to the lives of ordinary people in his church, invited the family of a young person who had died to come and join him around the coffin and hold hands – acknowledging unity with the one who had gone, and in support of one another.
- A friend shared with me the story of how her husband died suddenly and unexpectedly on the summit of Mt Snowdon in Wales. One year later, she and her family and friends retraced the last climb he had made with his wife and children before his death. They stopped on their journey and she spoke of the love that they had shared together as husband and wife, and how they had exchanged wedding rings as a token of that love. She spoke also of the love he had for his two daughters, and then she presented each of them with their own gold ring which she had had made from their father's wedding ring, to remind them of his continuing love. We can either let life destroy us, or allow the experience to be transforming – and ritual is a key factor in that.

- After the passing of someone, whether close or less well
  known, there will come a time such as looking at the Christmas card list when their loss is brought again to mind. The
  list will have to be adjusted – but rather than just a hasty
  pressing of the delete button, make it a special moment to
  remember them, give thanks, and perhaps also write a note
  to the one who will be missing them most. Pray for them.
  Maybe create in your computer a special folder in which you
  record the particular wisdom they brought to you. If you
  don't easily work with a computer then make a memory
  book to include photos and other artefacts.

Such simple actions can be profoundly meaningful when words
fail us. Perhaps each family member taking a single flower and
laying it on a grave may be more meaningful than a lot of flowers
sent anonymously by a florist – because it allows those grieving
to do something. Maybe in due course, planting the seeds of wild
flowers over the grave will be a reminder of resurrection. Or if
you have space, planting a species tree will not only be a beautiful reminder but will also encourage you to keep looking
upwards to your source of hope. The natural world is a constant
reminder of rebirth and new life: the certainty that the death of
winter is followed by the emergence of spring, growing into
the abundance of summer and eventual harvest in autumn
encourages us to hope.

'Except a corn of wheat falls into the ground and dies it
abides alone but if dies it brings forth much fruit.'[8] These words,
spoken and written centuries ago, echo the truth that death is not
the end but is merely a passage to some other realm where we
will reach fulfilment. As a more recent slogan puts it, 'we are not
human beings having a spiritual experience, but spiritual beings
having a human experience'. None of this makes the parting
easier, but it does allow us to express our emotions, which is part
of being human. Remember that tears are like jewels, expressing
our love for the person who has moved to another spiritual state,
and in shedding those tears we begin to encounter healing of our

spirit. If ashes are to be scattered, then choose a place of meaning to you and the person who has died. Never do it in a hurry, and always imagine in advance how you want this to happen: what you want to say and do, the words you might include, the aspirations you might express. Do you want to be alone? If others are to come, choose them with care: this is not a time to allow yourself to be manipulated by other people's preferences.

Even in the midst of the most emotionally painful committal services I have ever been involved in, the words from the Gospel never fail to impact me powerfully: 'I am the resurrection and the life, those who believe in me though they were dead yet shall they live.'[9] It is on such an occasion when all hope is apparently gone that those who have nurtured their spirituality find a source of inner strength that defies unbelief.

As a well spent day brings happy sleep, so life well used brings happy death.

Leonardo da Vinci, Italian artist & engineer (1452–1519)

CHAPTER THREE

Times
and
Seasons

The Days of Our Life

Everything that happens has happened before;
nothing is new, nothing under the sun.
(Ecclesiastes 1:9, Contemporary English Version)

Every Day

Sometimes we describe ourselves in relation to times of the day – a 'morning person' or a 'night person'. It may correlate with different personality types, or maybe it relates to how our lifestyles require us to be. Whatever the reason, the beginning and ending of each day are important times. Morning people may take longer with their rising rituals, while evening people give more time and reflection to the end of the day. Monastic life is focused on a daily rhythm: doing things in a set order, and knowing what will happen, and when, gives structure to daily existence. Even in a hectic 24/7 lifestyle, it is natural to wish for the sense of stability and meaning which a structured daily routine can offer.

Our ancient forebears had no choice but to live by the natural rhythm of light and darkness. Technology now allows us to create any environment we wish at the touch of a button, and it can be difficult to find moments of stillness. As a result, we are often less well prepared than we need to be when something unexpected comes along. Teachers tell me that when the day is clearly structured, young children settle into it very easily, and those who care for the elderly find the same is true for them. It seems that we can cope with changes in routine just as long as we know what to expect.

In Asia it is not uncommon to see workers out in open spaces early in the morning, practicing martial arts, yoga, and other focusing disciplines as a way of preparing for the day ahead. The Christian tradition has always encouraged setting aside a time to meditate and pray at the start of each day. In a climate that is generally sunny or warm all year, then a brisk walk, a run or a jogging routine may make good sense, whereas those who live in a less predictable climate are more likely to find that something that can be done indoors will be more effective. Whatever you do, a morning ritual should be appropriate to the context of your overall lifestyle. If your day is likely to be noisy and stressful then meditation, prayer, reading or journaling may be good options – though avoid things that would naturally calm the body down ready for sleep, unless you have been out working all night, of course! In the morning, you need to get ready to meet the new day.

Whatever you choose, there is a need to find the spiritual sustenance that will enable us to tap into that wisdom which will nurture our daily lives. A morning ritual does not need to be something additional to what you might otherwise do, and can be constructed around things like eating breakfast, taking vitamins, brushing teeth, washing, dressing, leaving the house, saying goodbye to family/house-mates, the journey to work, and more. The Hebrew people had passages of their scriptures attached to the door posts so that each time they passed through they could reflect on them.[1]

At the end of the day, we need to reflect on what is past. Make time to write, draw, paint or make a journal entry,[2] maybe using the reflections as a way into meditation or prayer. Light candles, burn incense, play quiet music. Make a note of things that need attention. Make that phone call. Plan what you will do about unfinished business. The old adage 'not to let the sun go down on your anger' is a healthy recipe for mind, body and spirit, and can save relationships from disintegrating as well as bringing peace of mind. Other things that can provide a focus for the day's ending are music, the last food or drink of the day, washing, taking medication, switching off the electricity and lights, locking the door, closing the curtains. These are simple actions, but the rhythm of some of them (such as a hot drink or warm bath) help to settle our bodies physically, while things like switching off electrical appliances will save us being restless and losing sleep worrying about them.

Every Week

The first day of a week is a time to plan things for the coming days. Post a list in a prominent place – maybe next to the mirror you use, or strategically placed on your notice-board. Don't set too many goals, but be realistic in what you think you can accomplish. Give yourself a new start – blank sheet. If you regularly use a computer it might be helpful to have a diary entry that appears at a specific time each week. Why not change your computer wallpaper to start the new week, or choose a different piece of music for each week to broaden your horizons.

At week's end, try to complete unfinished tasks such as phone calls or emails. List things which are still incomplete, and note how you will tackle them next week. Why not make the equivalent of a weather map of your week with those colourful papers that have sky or landscape scenes, and use symbols depicting how things have been (sun, clouds, rain, storm, etc.). This can be a group activity, with others who live in the same house, or indeed any group of friends. Since children can easily participate, it makes an ideal family activity. Talk about the week, help one another to see things in perspective: congratulate or encourage, offer help in resolving problems. Using symbols allows people to articulate as much or as little as they are comfortable with, so if in a group try not to force discussion of issues prematurely but be content with creating a safe space where in due course it will be possible to talk.

If you are combining this with your own end of day routine, then acknowledge your achievements in your meditation. If you use oils or incense each day, then use a different one for the end of a week. You might take a bath or shower to wash away the things you want to be rid of – you could add quiet music, perhaps a glass of wine, and especially candles as a symbol of light and hope. As you begin to explore new ways of marking occasions, you will find other things that will work for you. My eldest son has an hour's drive home from work, and on Fridays he takes a different route, marking the beginning of special time with his wife and children.

EVERY MONTH

On the first day, turn the calendar. Choose one with pictures that feed your spirit – a humorous one if you take yourself too seriously. Setting goals for the month reminds us of medium-term intentions: planning ahead like this avoids that last-minute rush when we have too much to do and not enough time. A monthly ritual might include buying and choosing cards for birthdays, anniversaries or special occasions, so they are delivered on time and invested with meaning. For an especially significant occasion, making your own card will say a lot because you have invested something of yourself in it. The most difficult thing can be knowing what to write in cards, so make a habit of collecting sayings and short phrases and then you will not be stuck for words.

Why not choose a different book to read each month or try out a new meal? Both of them could be done with a group of friends who share their ideas.

At month's end, take time to reflect. Use a graph,[3] or try a monthly weather map to show the trends. This helps to keep things in perspective: you can't have a storm force wind every day! Sharing this ritual with a group can be therapeutic: those who've had a sunny month/week can bless and encourage those whose life has been stormy. Mathematical types could create a balance sheet. Viewing the negatives and positives this way can open windows onto different ways of viewing life.

A typical monthly balance sheet

Blessings (Credit)	Problems (Debit)
Partner	Stress
Children	Long work hours
Friends	Lifestyle imbalance
Cash in the bank	Debt
Home	Difficult relationships
Work	Erratic life style
Hobbies	
Health	Illness
Holidays	
Recreation	
Leisure	Not enough time
Community	Loneliness
Faith	Doubt

EVERY YEAR

If you keep a journal, be sure to get your new book in good time. Decorate the first page with your aspirations for the year ahead. Invite the folk with whom you celebrate the New Year to sign the first page. Whatever you do, don't miss the first day as that sets the tone for the rest of the year. If you don't like writing, collages or graphs offer different creative ways to accomplish the same end. Or capture the year in photographs: take a specific one each week or month that sums up what is going on in your life. And of course, on the first of every year there is always a new calendar to be opened and hung up prominently. To address the challenge of staying with your ambitions, make a pact with a friend: write your goals down and get her to mail them to you every month, or once a quarter. You can do the same in return: it can be a good reminder if you don't let it become just one more thing that has to be done. If you're too private for that, then set your computer diary up to remind you regularly.

At year's end, review your journal and take time to highlight your achievements. Check out things you would like to change in the coming year. Review your graphs. Does your life go through cycles? If a meeting at work always creates gale force images, or an engagement with a particular person fills you with apprehension, or (for women) if PMS coincides with clouds on the weather map – then knowing this means you can do something about it. Write down the things you want to ditch from the year – and burn or shred the paper. This is a great time to clear out things you no longer need but which could find new life at the thrift store. And deal with unfinished business: make that awkward phone call, or write that difficult letter before the year is out. But remember that dealing with guilt doesn't mean offloading it onto someone else. If there is an ongoing issue, then talk to a counsellor and work through it rather than allowing it to disempower you.

Light a candle and burn some incense to take you symbolically through from one year to the next. Let it be your guiding light of promise and hope.

A New Year's Prayer

As I/we pass from the old year (20xx) to the New Year (20xx) I leave behind the failures and the things that have gone wrong. Sometimes I've been to blame, and for those I seek forgiveness: where I have been wronged I refuse to hold anger. By

2: PERSONAL TIMES

Anniversaries can be a mixed blessing. They remind us that the years are slipping away, but it's good to celebrate even the small anniversaries as a way of giving thanks and appreciating the bigger perspective of life's journey. There is something very special about being remembered on a significant occasion, and if you're giving a gift it is worth thinking outside the box and getting something that really suits the recipient's needs. On my first wedding anniversary I remember going into the medical school where I worked and an older woman (who was desperate to know if I was still in love) greeted me with, 'Well, did you get a bunch of roses then?' The answer was, 'No, I got a washing machine.' At the time, my husband was a full-time student and washing machines were proportionately expensive – and this was a second-hand reconditioned model — but it transformed our lifestyle, and no washing machine was ever loved so much!

Some anniversaries are hard to face. The first year following a death is one endless list of significant anniversaries, and it is important to take time to process this because it is hard to reinvent life until that year is lived through. Writing a journal through the whole year of emotions and feelings can help, as can revisiting previous years. One widow I know decided to read through all the journals that she and her husband had kept over the years, and then at the end of the year to dispose of them, signifying her readiness to move on.

If you already do something creative such as painting or writing poetry, or some other hands-on hobby, then picking it up may help you to express some of your inner emotions which in turn may help you to engage again with life. If you don't have a creative outlet, then consider joining a group to try something new. It makes no difference how skilled you are (though most people are more gifted than they believe): the important thing is the way such activities facilitate our inner journey to peace. In the process, you will likely find new friends as well as new interests.

Birthdays

These ideas could be used on any birthday:

- *Annual photo* – most children have an annual class photograph in school, but you can create one in the family as well. Once a birthday photo is integrated into the regular annual cycle, children will tend to remind you of its importance – and you have a simple ritual around which stories can be told and memories created. Sending the picture along with a thank-you email can also soon become a ritual for such occasions.
- *Ring chimes* or a bell – or pop champagne — at the actual time of birth.
- *Cards* – choose your favourite card each year, and mount it in a book or file.
- *Keep a special birthday box* and add something significant from each year to your box.

First birthdays are always special. Photos are especially important in the early years because children change so quickly. If you are keeping a personal box you will already be collecting memorable items.[5] One of my friends keeps a box for each of his godchildren, adding news items and photos from their birthdays each year, which he will then present to them when they reach the grown-up age of 18 or 21 as a record of the world they have lived through. Keeping birthday cards in a scrap-book is another great way to record a child's personal history. Why not make a recording of the conversation around the table – unobtrusively, of course, so everyone acts naturally? This can be great fun to listen to in later years.

    Birthdays between one and five are all quite special and offer opportunities to help a child to feel easy with being the centre of attraction. Enabling a child to accept praise, gifts and compliments without embarrassment is an important part of growing up. In time they will recognize that other people have special days too, and that also is important for a child's development so that they learn to see themselves in community and appreciate that the world doesn't revolve around their personal needs. For our children to grow up to be whole people, nurturing their spiritual life is just as important as ensuring that they have all their childhood inoculations. Spiritual awareness is not measured by reference to cognitive skills. There is an appropriate spiritual response for a three-year-old that is as valid for them as the quite different way a thirty-year-old might respond. Human development is a bit like the growth of a tree. The sapling with only a few rings is no less a tree than a huge specimen with hundreds of rings. Given the appropriate circumstances for growth, the sapling has the potential for the same level of development.[6] Children are by nature intuitive, so the environment we create will either nourish them or stultify them. They absorb atmosphere, and the experience is never neutral: they will be affected one way or the other, for good or ill. A child who is introduced to the wonders of nature will grow up understanding the importance of caring for the world around them, and the same is true of human relationships. Although children think concretely rather than abstractly this does not mean they cannot have spiritual experiences. In his book *The Spirit of the Child* educational researcher David Hay suggests that children have an innate spirituality which is often destroyed by adult responses.[7]

Turning five is usually a significant step, often associated with going to school and starting to grow up, which is still special even for children who have had experience of pre-school nursery or daycare. Mark the transition by giving some 'grown up' things like pencils, notebook, purse, bag, even a first journal with blank pages to stick things in and draw in. Design the first page with the child, including thumb, finger, hand or even foot prints. Knowing that they are special – unique – will build them up and give them confidence.

Double figures: I always remember a boy who played with

my son telling me that he would be allowed to stay up late to go to the Christmas Eve midnight service when he 'got into double figures'. He repeated this regularly, and I remember thinking that his parents had found a novel way to ensure he did things at an appropriate age, acknowledging that at an earlier stage he would have been unable to cope with a late night on Christmas Eve, while also creating an aspiration for him as he grew up.

Thirteen: dawn of the teenage years. Perhaps best acknowledged by giving a degree of responsibility such as managing an allowance for clothes, or allocating a household chore which can have some remuneration (not necessarily a cash benefit). This sort of ritual (which may well already have started with a small regular allowance and packing their own school bag) can take on increased importance as the young person has a growing realization of being an integral part of the family community. Though the idea might initially be resisted, giving teenagers household responsibilities will provide a sense of security at a time when much else is changing. The responsibility can be increased as they prove themselves competent and reliable. They won't get it perfect (did you?) so don't go over the top if they mess up sometimes, but work with them to get back on track. If they do fail, they will probably be angrier at themselves than you are, so be sensitive.

Eighteen/Twenty-one: Different cultures mark one or other of these birthdays as signs of maturity, traditionally symbolized in the giving of a key to the door of the family home. Today's children have a key long before this time, but still enjoy the significance of the symbol. It is often better to mark the occasion with different events for different groups: one for family and friends and another with their peers. Marking these times need not be expensive: it is the observance of them that is important. This one is especially important because it is now the only event left to Western young people that comes anywhere near to being a 'rite of passage'. So choose symbols that will mean something. A woman I met recently in California told me what she did for her daughter and son when they reached eighteen. Her daughter received an apron with the strings cut off, but folded in the pocket – indicating that she had grown up but there would always be a lifeline connecting her to home whenever it may be required. She gave her son a battery with jump leads – symbolizing that he had grown up, but she was there for him whenever he needed her.

This is also an appropriate time to give a photo album which spans the life of the young person and those important to her or him. There is definitely something particularly beautiful about a nice album, but an up-to-date version might be a CD.

If as a young person you have no family who are going to do this for you, then make it a personal project. Find photos of yourself and retrieve information from wherever you can of your history and make a scrap-book of your life. If there are not many photos you can also find cards, newspapers, magazines that celebrate the happenings on a given date which you might want to include. You need to take special care in doing this, because if you have to do it yourself then some support networks are probably not working for you. Remember that you are special because you are made in the image of God: you are a creative person. As someone made in God's image you need to start seeing yourself the way God sees you and according to the Bible story, God saw everything that was made and thought, 'This is good'.[8] Another poet addresses God with these words: 'You created my inmost being; you knit me together in my mother's womb.'[9]

When I was a boy of fourteen, my father was so ignorant I could hardly stand having the old man around. But when I got to be twenty-five, I was astonished at how much the old man had learned.

Mark Twain, American writer (1835–1910)

Thirty: Perhaps this is the occasion to present the birthday box mentioned earlier, containing a treasure stored from each year of childhood. Having been kept over the years by a loving parent, it is now definitely the adult's responsibility. You can of course give it at 21 or 18 but at those ages many young people find themselves still not settled in what they consider a permanent home, in which case it is probably better to hang on to it. Just make sure it is handed over at a significant time, and thirty seems to be an age when many people review what they have accomplished and plan where they might go next. It is not too late to make even major changes of career or lifestyle, so encourage them to consider a regular evaluation along the lines of some of the suggestions at the start of this chapter.

Forty: This time has been significant for many years and it is particularly nice to have a party thrown for you rather than organizing it yourself. You will encourage this to happen if you have been generous in your celebration of other people's birthdays. If not, just drop a few broad hints.

Fifty: Look at your achievements and decide to make life changes that you see as significant. If there is something you have always wanted to do, this is the time to do it. If not, find something that is new to you, that is achievable, and that you will be able to pursue in the future. Be intentional about refusing to become old prematurely. Connecting with other people can prevent depression – and if you have been nurturing your spirituality you will be finding that, far from feeling life is all downhill now, you are actually exploring new dimensions of being.

Sixty: You may have been considering what to do in retirement, thinking about where to live and the kind of home that will be suitable. In today's global village, many folk find that their families and close friends live further away than they would like. Let modern technology work for you. If you are not already hooked up to email, then do it now and get daily access to keep in touch with anyone anywhere in the world. A woman I know who was widowed in her early sixties was suddenly traumatized by yet another son moving to live overseas with his family, and was persuaded to get a computer and email. It transformed her of us should have a small book or journal to hand just for these special occasions. But one thing we can all do is give thanks.

Gardeners probably notice the changing seasons more easily than others, but we are all connected to the rhythm of the earth by the seasons. Wall-to-wall sunshine throughout the year may seem appealing, but those who have to live with it are deprived of the diversity that changing seasons give. Variation helps to regulate the speed of life. Technology tends to subvert this natural rhythm, allowing us to create light at the flick of a switch, and providing transportation and refrigeration that makes the same foods available all year round. We all appreciate these advantages, but when we lose touch with the cycle of the seasons because of such modern luxuries there is the associated danger of disconnecting from the natural world. By the use of rituals we can begin to reconnect with our environment. The simplest ritual is the bringing into the home of flowers, fruits or evergreen branches to mark and celebrate the seasonal change. Creating a space in the home could be as simple as having a vase on a windowsill or an elaborate hall dressing. A significant change can take place at each season. Change fresh blossoms each week, or if choosing a plant then the watering will be the weekly ritual. While paying attention to the flowers and fruits, pray, reflect or use a mantra to nurture this spiritual moment.

The garden provides a variety of approaches to nurture our spirituality. Weeding can help us work through small problems, while double digging really enables us to address the bigger challenges. Like spring cleaning, gardening creates space to sort everything out, from daily occurrences to major life events. The answer to an apparently insoluble situation can fall into place quite simply after a day in the garden. This is probably what inspired the statement that 'One is nearer to God in the garden than anywhere else on earth'.

Gardening brings us closer to memories as well. Working with plants that began as cuttings given by friends allows time to think about them. Some people may have died, and I lovingly cherish their memories; others I see only occasionally, and I catch up with my thoughts about them and voice a prayer. Other plants remind me of events that have taken place in the garden, and which inspire me to thanksgiving. By the end of a gardening day, I may be tired and ready to crash out with music, a candle, or incense – certainly a bath – but the process has been empowering. Being in a garden can draw us close to the rhythm of the environment, but we have to be intentional about this and self-consciously allow nature to feed our spirits: it was through neglect of this that some of our forebears found it so easy to rape and pillage the environment, the consequences of which we live with today.

Do me a favour during the rainy season,
and I shall do the same for you during
the dry season.

African proverb

SPRING

I absolutely love spring-cleaning. There is always one day when the winter sun seems to gather strength and suddenly I see things I hadn't noticed in the darker days of winter. I enjoy the sheer physical effort of serious cleaning, and I love to throw open the windows and let the fresh air in. This is a good time to reassess the things that have worked their way to the back of drawers and cupboards, to clear out clutter and reorganize things, wash doors and windows, clean furnishings and repair broken things, to move furniture around and rediscover lost items. I find that doing this gives me the chance to reappraise how much junk I have collected in my life. I get the opportunity to work on my goals – but the interesting thing is that I never consciously set out to do this, for me it just happens in the process. So at the end of a day of spring-cleaning I like to take a bath and wash away the physical dirt and lay to rest my mind's clutter, and dress in

beach somewhere else. The water lapping at my feet had almost
certainly travelled past my home in the northern hemisphere at
some stage in its long history. The ebbing and flowing of the
tides allows us to connect with our fellow human beings across
the world. Using this consciously can create a space for us to
engage with some of the world's big issues, such as violence,
greed, or poverty. Even walking the beach can become a ritual
full of purpose and meaning, if we intentionally engage with
reflections of this sort (and no doubt many others).

Autumn

The gathering of the harvest and the shortening of daylight hours
can be just as inspirational as the lengthening of spring days if
used intentionally, by pruning, harvesting, taking cuttings, stack-
ing logs, making bark chippings and compost, working with
nature in the recycling process. All these activities give opportunities for us to reflect on the value of working with the seasons,
being good stewards, facilitating a sense of hope for the future as
we plant bulbs for the following year. The actual planting can
become a ritual itself. When the bulbs come up after the waiting
period we cannot help but reflect back to when we were planting
and consider how sometimes what seemed like insurmountable
problems have been resolved and how the divine power has sustained us. A walk in the country takes on a new hue. I remember
one year when we were especially short of cash, we collected
autumn leaves and pressed them to create Christmas gifts, selecting colours and textures that we felt matched their recipients, or
our relationship with them.

Leisure time at this season is often taken up with repair
jobs around the house, making the place secure before winter
sets in, clearing fallen leaves out of roof guttering and drainage
pipes. Then there is the final cutting of lawns and hedges, the
pruning of shrubs and trees, and the smell of wood smoke from
the garden bonfire. Even if you have no garden, the same thing
happens in public parks, and there too the signs of the season can

evoke spiritual enquiry. I still have vivid memories of one of my children at about two or three years old kicking a pile of leaves in a park and then asking, 'Daddy, do you think God is at the bottom of everything?'

WinTER

It can seem like death has surrounded us, but anyone who has woken up to the surprise of a hard frost or unexpected snowfall will know the clarification and new definition that appears as branches and twigs are etched in frost. We see things differently. While the ground is cold it is a suitable time to move large plants with deep roots or to plant a new shrub or tree, offering the chance to contemplate changes and adjustments we may need to make in other areas of life. This season also offers a sense of hope and anticipation for the future. There is indeed an existential dimension to gardening. The dark months are not wasted as we repair sheds and invest time in somewhat less appealing jobs. Those who think ahead and get their tools cleaned and sharpened find they can get it done easily now, without the long delays there might be in spring or summer. Cold short days offer opportunities to repair paths and fences. All these jobs offer space for intentional reflection to relate the activity to our spiritual concerns. Working with the seasons means that we can cover each area of life with repeated regularity, thereby preventing imbalance. The very fact that in winter the days are shorter emphasizes the importance of taking adequate time for rest. Learning the different ways of multiplying plants, whether from cuttings, by division, from seed or layering, reminds us of the infinite variety of the human race. Just like plants, people are different and need personal attention. One size does not fit all, whether in life or in the garden.

A larger space, perhaps communal to several homes, offers the opportunity to create a garden that will enhance a neighbourhood. This could also bring together the skills of a group to make a garden that could include a labyrinth or a Zen garden. The process in itself will nurture a sense of community, while the construction of a living labyrinth will automatically create opportunities for talking about ritual and encouraging others to take part, as people walk through responding to the sights and sounds around them.

A personal winter ritual

Winter means different things in different countries, but even in warm climates there is a nostalgic attraction to pictures of snow and ice, so you could use this winter ritual wherever you live. Take a picture of yourself and place it in a clear container (choose one with straight sides, and flexible plastic rather than glass). Fill it with water and then place it in the freezer (or, if you live in a genuinely cold place, put it outside overnight). When you take it out you will see yourself set in ice. Remove the ice from its container and place it on a plate big enough to catch the melting ice. Put it on a table in front of you. Slowly watch it melt, and as it does so, pray that those experiences in your life which have left you feeling cold and frozen will melt with the ice. Let them go, and finally retrieve the picture from the water and blot it dry before mounting it in your journal, or framing it to remind you regularly of this cathartic experience. Allow yourself the freedom to melt and begin to enjoy the world again. Like winter, you will soon turn the corner and be approaching a new springtime, offering fresh opportunities for growth and development.

CHAPTER FOUR

EVERYDAY LIFE

Never lose an opportunity of seeing
anything that is beautiful; for beauty is
God's handwriting - a wayside
sacrament. Welcome it in every fair face,
in every fair sky, in every fair flower, and
thank God for it as a cup of blessing.

Ralph Waldo Emerson, American poet and philosopher
(1803–82)

1: PLACES

HOMES AND GARDENS

Most people have several homes and gardens in the course of a lifetime. Our first home as independent adults is always going to be a place of learning and, eventually, of memories. It is worthwhile thinking about relevant rituals at this time, as the move into your first home will probably coincide with a significant stage in life, and creating intentional rituals at this stage will be a long-lasting gift of memories.

In moving from one house to another, it is important to close down the old home as well as opening up the new, affirming the memories of what is passing while also welcoming the future. Here are a few ideas:

- Make a mosaic that encapsulates memories or images of the old house to take with you, and then make a corresponding one of the new house, this time incorporating your hopes and aspirations.
- You could embed a key from each house in the mosaic. Or create an outline of the old and new houses, divided down the centre, with one side representing the old, and the other half the new – again using intentional symbols to link past and future.
- Instead of mosaic choose another medium that you are more familiar with such as cross stitch, patchwork, or pastels. Think laterally.
- Choose some stones from the garden of the old house or its nearby community, etching or writing words or symbols on them that sum up your feelings about the old house. Using stone highlights the permanence of the memories. You can arrange the stones attractively in a special place in your new home or garden, and as your life develops in the new environment add other stones to your collection, indicating your gradual transition to the point where you feel that this now really is a place to call 'home'.

For a moving-in ritual, how about choosing a large candle, then lighting it and moving with the light through each room and passageway of the new house. Work out in advance who will use each room, and what they will typically do there, so that as you go you can consciously invite the divine spirit to inhabit the space.

- At the main entrance you may ask that light will welcome all who enter, and guide their path as they leave.
- In the kitchen you may ask for nourishment of your body and a building of community.
- In the sitting area or lounge you may ask that the sharing of stories will bring wisdom to those who live there.

- In the bedrooms, that rest and relationships may be deepened.
- In bathrooms or showers, that cleansing and renewing of spirit might never dry up.
- In the garden, patio, or balcony that all leisure and work may enrich our lives.

The ancient Hebrew people fixed words from their sacred writings on their doorpost, and orthodox Jews still have a Mezuzah (Hebrew word for doorpost) by a home's entrance.[1] It contains a small parchment scroll inscribed on one side with the Biblical passages Deuteronomy 6:4–9 and 11:13–21. You might like to do something similar: in a space near to the door, fix a plaque with words of wisdom that will inspire your daily journeys. As with any ritual, just putting words on the doorpost could be a meaningless exercise if you then rush past it. But if you pause to consider the words as you leave and enter the home this simple action can be infused with deep meaning. This can also be a means of introducing even quite young children to the importance of paying attention to their spiritual development.

The garden has become a significant space in our homes, and we avidly watch TV programmes about creating and remodelling them (and 'garden' in this context means any outdoor space, ranging from a landscaped patch to a corner of a small balcony). In the past, a garden was a place for growing things, but today's garden designers emphasize the creation of spaces where people can relax, meditate, read, and be intentional in building relationships with family, neighbours and friends – in other words, sacred or spiritual spaces where ritual finds a natural home. Few of us can afford professional makeovers, so we have to create such spaces for ourselves. In doing this, remember that gardens don't look after themselves, and there will always be watering, weeding, and the controlling of pests. But none of these things need be a burden if you intentionally create rituals around them (for this, see the section on the seasons of nature in the previous chapter). Whether creating a garden from nothing or remodelling an existing garden, you are bound to express something of who you are. But it also offers possibilities for exploring new ways of being. A garden always presents a significant perspective on time: nothing grows overnight, and what one person plants another generation will see in all its full glory. There can be more instant rewards, though, in the colourful displays that can be created by the use of annuals in just a few weeks during the summer. Features such as wind chimes, bird tables, ponds or sculptures all expand the possibilities for spiritual creativity. The scope for meaningful design in the garden is limited only by the imagination, and is a unique form of partnership with the Creator.

WORK SPACE

We make a living by what we get, we make a life by what we give.
    Sir Winston Churchill, British politician (1874–1965)

Large numbers of people find themselves cash-rich but time-poor, and the reason is our love affair with work. Many people work longer hours than they theoretically should, and recent research has shown that significant numbers of workers never even take their full entitlement of annual leave. A spirituality of time is especially important in this context. Placing a clock might therefore be a highly appropriate ritual for a new office or place of work. It is very easy to let work take more of our time than it deserves, and when that happens it has consequences for the rest of life. It is simple enough to buy a clock, but how about making one for your own space? Doing so will certainly add to its significance, and also offer an opportunity to reflect on the nature of time, and the way we use it. You can purchase the works for a clock from any craft supplier, and then mount it on a tile which can be bought from a hardware store. A plain one gives scope for painting your own design and numbers with ceramic paint.

Mixing 'work' with 'leisure' in this way raises interesting questions about the nature of these two activities: are they really as separate and disconnected as our culture has made them, or is there not an intrinsic connection between the two, in which they are but two sides of the one coin that is the process of everyday living? Having created a timepiece, think carefully about where to place it, in a position so that others as well as you can see it. At the same time you might also compose some words that sum up your approach to work, perhaps including your mission statement. If colleagues work together on this, it will be more significant. Think of ways to display the words, whether on the wall or computer screen.

A collage made as a group could serve the same purpose. If you are moving to a new location with other colleagues, you might each think of making or choosing something suitable and mark this new beginning by affirming your commitment to work in peace and harmony with one another. There might be a place for something that symbolically connects the space to the type of work that happens there: for example, lawyers might display some old-fashioned scales of justice, while plumbers might incorporate a small water feature, and so on. It is also worth thinking about a weekly ritual, for instance by different workers introducing a new display of fresh flowers each Monday morning thereby bringing a touch of the natural world into what might otherwise be an austere and technical atmosphere with no access in many cases even to outside light. An equivalent daily ritual might be to have fresh fruit in a bowl for people to help themselves, rather than the usual chocolate biscuit. These are small things encouraging people to live and work in harmony with one another, adding to the sum total of their happiness and job satisfaction – and also their efficiency as workers.

Increasing numbers of people work from home, or spend significant parts of their working time doing so. Many homes now have a space designated as an 'office' to deal with all the paperwork that seems to be an inescapable factor of life today. One of the challenges in this situation is developing the ability to create a clearly defined working area so that work does not over-run the whole of life. Even if there are limited resources, creating a space that is pleasing will encourage you in your work and reflect the value you put on yourself and what you do. More of us are coming to recognize that all of life is spiritual, and that can give us a new understanding of work, in which it will not be a drudgery but might even become, as Martin Luther said, 'prayer' or 'worship'. A ritual to start or end the day is particularly valuable when you work at home, and can become the equivalent of a daily journey to and from another workplace. Many home workers use computers, and an appropriate daily ritual might include exploring one of the many websites that offer interactive spiritual reflections, or registering with a site which will send a regular inspirational piece of wisdom direct to your email.[2] For additional fun, how about starting each new week by changing the appearance of the desktop on your computer? Link it to the seasons, your family or friends, the environment, or something that you want to be spiritually intentional about this week. Add some inspirational words to the wallpaper screen to encourage you each time you log on.

2: Waking, Eating and Sleeping

When you arise in the morning, give
thanks for the morning light, for your
life and strength. Give thanks for your
food, and the joy of living. If you see no
reason for giving thanks, the fault lies
with yourself.
    Tecumseh, Native American Shawnee Chief (1768–1813)

Many regular routines are necessary just to keep life ticking over, and they can easily become boring and tedious. Rituals will not solve this, but they can certainly help.

SHOWERING/BRUSHING TEETH/COMBING HAIR/POLISHING SHOES

All these activities focus on preparing for the day ahead, and giving time to them underlines to you that you care about yourself, and that what you are going to do is of real importance. You need to love yourself before you can love the rest of the world, including especially the people you live, work or play with. A friend of mine uses coloured spots placed strategically alongside the places where these activities take place, and then uses them intentionally as a reminder to pray or reflect on some particular issue or theme. This can be an opportunity to focus on a mantra that directs you to any special concern you may have.

EATING

Taking food is essential to keep our bodies working efficiently, and how we do that is a ritual just waiting to happen. We all know that if we graze on snacks throughout the day we are unlikely to end up with a balanced diet. This can lead to obesity on the one hand and eating disorders on the other. St Paul described our bodies as 'temples', a place where the divine chooses to dwell, and if we regard ourselves in this light we will be less abusive of ourselves. Even governments are becoming concerned about the lack of essential nutrients in much of what we eat, but it can be hard to change long-standing habits. Let a ritual help here. Think about one day at a time. On waking, take a drink of plain water to start the day, and consciously decide 'today I will eat wisely'. Water is essential to life and most of us drink a lot less than we should, so regular glasses of water can become a way of reminding ourselves of our aspirations throughout the day.

Create a meal plan for the week ahead. As you compile the list of ingredients let this become a ritual in itself, and then be intentional in sticking to the list when you go shopping. Think ahead. Will you be eating out? Could you pack a lunch? This

them to make it and hang it above their bed. Use it as a sign that you are asking for a peaceful night's sleep free from anxiety and fear.

3: REDEEMING THE ROUTINES

We all have things that need to be done on a regular basis – things like changing a drinking water filter, filling up the screen wash on your car, or checking the tyre pressure. Some typical examples follow, but the list could be endless. Identify your own routines, and then decide which ones you will intentionally use as opportunities for engagement with the deeper aspects of life.

BUSINESS CARDS

In the west we often just take a card and with a cursory glance stuff it in a pocket or file. The Japanese accompany the exchange of business cards with very extensive protocols and while those particular rituals may not appeal to everyone, this is part of modern life which could be invested with meaning by an intentional action. By carefully reading the card and making eye contact with the giver, you will be acknowledging their uniqueness and their innate spiritual value. In turn, they will probably be taken aback by the consideration being given to them, and in the process you may create a space that enables others also to reflect on who they truly are.

CARS

My husband's grandfather had very elaborate rituals for 'putting his car to bed'. His wife was disabled and the car was her lifeline to the outside world: both car and wife were treated with the same high regard. On any occasion when the car had been splashed with rain, or accumulated dust, it had to be cleaned and polished before it could be pushed (never driven) into the garage.

Once safely inside, it was tucked up with blankets and cloths to keep it warm, dry and clean. Before we were married, we occasionally borrowed this car, and the effort of all this ritual was one thing we did not look forward to. On reflection, though, it did have its value. For grandfather, it offered a reflective space to relive the events of the day, and to contemplate the car's main purpose in the scheme of his life. He never used it to go to work or to buy groceries, only to take his wife out for a ride. If your garage has space for the car, some similar ritual might well be worth thinking about, not only offering space to think about life, but to value material possessions, consider how we use them and also how much we spend on them.

Getting a new car usually involves losing one in order to gain another. Keep a picture of the car you are disposing of, including one showing you in it. You might want to keep a key and make a collection of the keys to all your cars over the years, which you can preserve in a box of memories. If your old car is to be scrapped, why not keep its number plate? If it is being sold on, take a rubbing of the number plate and then use these items in your collection of personal memorabilia. Getting to know a new car is like forging a new relationship. In fact, a car can be an extension of yourself, so you will want to wash and polish it regularly. I know quite a few people who always choose a name for their car, and have a naming ceremony when they bless the driver and all who will be driven in it. Buy a new piece of music specifically for this car, and maybe do it the honour of upgrading your driving skills by taking an advanced driving test if you have not already done that. At the very least, get an up-to-date edition of the Highway Code and read it carefully: you will be surprised at how much might have changed since the last time you did this. Clean out your garage to receive its new occupant, even paint the doors. Take a picture: you will part with it one day, and you will then have a first and a last photograph. And never forget that the dangers surrounding road travel are high: we need to do all we can towards ensuring our safety, and we need to engage our guardian angel.

A driver's prayer

As I drive today, may I drive with the spirit of the highway code and not just the rules.

Help me to be considerate to other drivers and pedestrians

Keep me from taking unnecessary risks and putting others' lives as well as my own at risk.

Protect me from unseen danger and let your angels guard me safely to my destination.

When I started doing research for this book, I was surprised how many people told me that they used their car as a key element in their daily ritual. I was living in southern California at the time, which is a very car-oriented culture, but I was still taken aback when friends told me they would drive round late at night as a way of relaxing after a stressful day. Some said they regularly drove up to a high vantage point (even the top of a multi-storey car park) for this purpose.

When I returned to Britain, I found people saying similar things. One family told me they regularly go for a drive if they are really angry with each other, explaining that since it is important to keep control of your emotions while driving, that discipline actually helps them to address other matters in a more reasonable fashion. This would be unlikely to work for everyone, but it works for them, and that is part of the secret with rituals: they need to work for you. Some people find it easier to talk about difficult things while driving – perhaps because by definition there is going to be no eye contact. Often people will talk about things to the driver, or the driver can ask questions in a way that seems less intrusive, and that enables the conversation. I remember one occasion when I had been driving through heavy traffic for over an hour. My passenger was a long-standing friend, who found that circumstance provided an appropriate opportunity to tell me that he was gay. There had been many previous conversations in which it would have been possible for him to have said that – but it was the car journey that offered a safe space for that statement to be made.

Dog Walking

A friend in California has a group of friends who all got dogs at about the same time. Instead of walking their dogs alone they arrange to meet up in the park. The dogs do their thing, and their owners talk. I remember a story told to me by Ian Fraser, a theologian who has collected stories of spiritual practices from base communities around the world. In one particular place where there was no sanitation, the women would meet every morning and sit around in a semicircle defecating and talking. When westerners brought modern sanitation to the community, that common meeting point was redundant, and its demise led to a significant diminution of community among those people.[5]

Emails

Who would have believed that such recently invented technology could become a daily ritual so quickly? In my family, collecting email is an integral part of the breakfast routine, no matter where in the world we might be at any given time. Being able to connect with people at the touch of a button is one of the modern technologies I regularly give thanks for. Why is it easier to type an email than write a letter? I don't know, but because it is, it lets us spread our generosity to a wider network and keep in touch with people who feel isolated. Use your inbox as an opportunity to remember the needs of those who write to you. And why not sign up for one of those daily emails that are offered by most newspapers, giving you the headlines – and creating another opportunity to hold the needs of the world before God.

Fitness

For a ritual to work well, it needs to fit into other aspects of our lifestyle. Gardening, housework, and DIY all provide exercise as well as a means of doing necessary work. Walking or cycling instead of driving, or climbing stairs instead of using the lift are other ways of building exercise into our daily routine. Keeping fit is essential to maintaining body, mind and spirit in harmony. The ancient Hebrews were exhorted to 'Love the Lord your God with all your heart, soul, mind and strength.'[6] This is a very holistic view of life, and includes all aspects of who we are. Someone who spends all their time studying and never exercising may have their head full of facts but be seriously obese. Or the other way round: an athletic body is not necessarily the sign of an active mind! And those who ignore or downplay the value of heart and soul will miss some of the most rewarding aspects of what it means to be truly human and fully alive. We all struggle to achieve a balanced lifestyle: you might like to take time to identify which of the sections in this book nurture your mind, body, heart and soul – and if you feel a weakness in one area, then that is an area you may need to work on especially. It is never too late to start to acquire some new skill. I only started in-line skating when I reached fifty, and I love it. Get the proper equipment and tuition, and make the care and choice of your gear a part of the ritual. Show yourself you are worth a little effort. Whatever your sport, include it in your journal.

For example a golfer might tape a golf tee into your journal to remind you that keeping a journal is not meant to become only a cerebral exercise. Or when playing a game of golf, allow yourself when placing the first and last tees to focus on bringing mind and body and spirit together in an act of intentional wholeness.

Jewellery

Because the wearing of jewellery is itself a regular ritual, it can be a particularly helpful way of nurturing spirituality. As I put my rings on each day, I recall specific aspects of life: my engagement ring, a statement of intentional commitment; my wedding ring, expressing a long and enduring commitment through good times and difficult times. Both the giving of the rings, and my wearing of them, are rituals speaking of and symbolizing a special relationship. One of my other pieces is newer than either of the rings: a handcrafted silver angel which I wear each day, intentionally acknowledging as I fasten it that I am opening myself to the divine spirit, inviting protection and guidance in everything I do and renewing my commitment to the one who gave it to me. Putting on a watch could also become a daily ritual linked to the ordering of our time.

In talking about this with one of my publishers, she pointed to her earrings and told me how they had been gifted to her when one of her close friends died. This friend had been a particular inspiration at a time when she felt her life was going nowhere, by encouraging her to initiate necessary changes even though she herself was terminally ill and had other things to bother about. She told me, 'Whenever I am commissioning a new book, or having a significant meeting, I always wear these now: my friend is still my continuing inspiration, and I want to honour the wisdom she gave me and live it out each day for her and for her family.'

Lights

Teaching children to switch lights on and off safely is to impart a basic life skill, but it can also be a ritual reminder of the importance of using the earth's resources wisely. When and how we do this is linked to the seasons and the latitude where we live. For those who are less mobile, the switching on of the evening light can be an important ritual marking the passage of days and seasons. The permanently housebound have many lonely hours to reflect, but the changes in the seasons do not pass by them unnoticed. If you know such a person you could encourage them in the creation of a ritual and reflection around these significant times of each day – or if you are reading this for yourself and your mobility is restricted in some way you might design a meaningful ritual for yourself and then share it with others whom you know.

Mail

I can still remember my father's letter opener and the methodical way he would first sort the mail by size into different piles, and then slit each envelope open before systematically reading the contents. For many of us, bills and other demands seem to be the only communications that have not yet succumbed to our love of email and text messaging. I often feel sorry for my own postal delivery people as they sometimes deliver more junk mail than anything that might be worth reading. When one receives a hand-written letter or personally designed card it is all the more special. With the rise in single person households and people who are isolated in their communities, the old-fashioned letter or card can be a means of affirming and nurturing one another's spirituality.

Newspapers and Magazines

There is scope here for a daily, weekly or monthly ritual depending on what you read. What do you do with the information once you have read it? Much of what we read will inform our worldview, and by carefully critiquing it we can then create an appropriate response which will become our ritual. Understanding what is going on in our communities will reflect on the quality of our citizenship only if we take action when that is appropriate. If someone you know has done well and it is reported in the papers, send them a card or note to encourage them. Use the hatch, match and dispatch columns to be a good neighbour. If you are in another country you might find yourself buying a paper or magazine from home just to keep you in touch with what is going on. It's amazing how even the tittle-tattle from home appeals when we are far away, causing us to acknowledge our roots. Theologian Karl Barth once said that 'We need to pray with the Bible in one hand and the newspaper in the other'. If I could organize it, this would be 'church' for me, especially on a Sunday when the papers are bigger and I sometimes have more time to read them. Discussion with other people, not just those who take my point of view, offers the opportunity to celebrate life, confess the wrongs both corporate and personal, to seek forgiveness, reflect on the opportunities presented, take notice of where God is at work in the world, identify how I might be part of that.

If you buy a craft or hobbies magazine, a ritual could be created by choosing one of the projects to complete each month, and don't forget that your papers and magazines form a useful resource for collage and journal work.

You could even make a ritual out of passing magazines on to someone who would not be able to afford them but would really value them – then eventually they can be recycled.

PERFUME

Working from home, I do not always wear make-up but I invariably use perfume. As I write, I have just finished a bottle, and I have a new one waiting to be opened. But that will be for tomorrow, because on that day I start a new job, working with people to nurture their spirituality. I want to start my new perfume then as an intentional commitment and prayer that I will bring divine fragrance into their lives, dispelling hostility and conflict.

Phones

Phones can be a nightmare or a blessing. It is the purpose of rituals to reduce the nightmares and increase the blessings: this is redemption, turning the nightmares around. Always pause before you answer the phone. Take a deep breath. It may save you answering hastily, to your subsequent regret. Refuse to be intimidated by whoever is at the other end: it is only a voice after all, it does not have power over you. No matter what another person may say, remember that 'a soft answer turns away wrath but grievous words stir up anger.'[7] You have the power to change the course of the conversation, possibly even of history. It is good to end a phone call with a blessing. Jewish people traditionally greet each other with 'shalom', which means more than the simple translation 'peace' – it is divine peace that promotes wholeness and well-being. If you close your conversation with that, it is always going to be more difficult to slam the phone down. And if the other person still does slam the phone down, that's not your problem.

Quality Time

An Australian family I knew created quality time with one another each Sunday evening by renting a video and eating fish and chips out of newspaper so that the time was spent with each other rather than in preparing and serving food. Even after their children had grown up they would still occasionally do this when they all returned to the family home. In this case, the ritual had provided built in memories, and a safe place to share with one another.

Nobody on his deathbed ever said, "I wish I had spent more time at the office".

Paul Tsongas, American politician (1941–97)

Scripture Reading

Where regular Bible reading has been separated from spiritual formation the practice has left many people asking, 'Why do this?' For the Bible to nurture our spirituality we need to engage with the text. First, a reliable text which reflects today's idiom is essential. In its day, the Bible was written in the language of the tabloids rather than the broadsheets, and large portions of it consist of the recording of oral traditions that were passed down in story form through many generations, while the poems were the songs and dances of a people who loved to celebrate. We are all aware of the way the Bible has at times been misused, whether by those pursuing their personal interests in war, or seeking to control women and others through the promotion of models of hierarchy and patriarchy, a process which did not nurture the spirit even of the perpetrators, let alone their victims. Yet the discovery of the person of Jesus in scripture is still a truly liberating spiritual experience. This story is having a huge impact on spiritual searchers, who often find themselves attracted to Jesus but with serious doubts about organized religion. By revisiting these ancient texts with new questions, we can unearth new and relevant meanings to renew our spirituality. Think of the questions you would like to ask of Jesus, and then read the gospels of the New Testament in that light. For example, a business person might wonder, 'What would Jesus look like as a relational leader?' or 'How did Jesus connect with people?' Surprising answers will emerge when we start to ask new questions.[8]

Shopping

Some people love it, and others hate it. Some go straight to the place where they will get what they want and then leave, while others like to browse. Some make a science out of shopping, while for others the real fun is the process of bartering. It is certainly fun to buy something new, and rewarding to find just the right thing that will light someone else's life up. But uncontrolled shopping can lead to the misery of overspending and waste.

Before shopping, think of spending in the context of your whole life and worldview. Can we really be concerned about world debt and then spend as though money was going out of fashion? Developing a spiritual focus will encourage wise stewardship of our resources by focusing on a global scale rather than simply on ourselves. Sit in a quiet place. Try visualizing four different ways you could spend the money you have available if you totally indulge yourself. Now think of four major projects around the world that need financial aid. Write down your needs (not your greeds), and then decide how to spend your money. It is not wrong to like nice things: a bereaved woman once told me that it was therapeutic for her to just go and look at the beautiful things in a particular shop, without having any need to buy them. Giving sacrificially can itself be a spiritual act that will nurture our beings, particularly if we refrain from advertising it to others. Jesus told many stories about money and its true value: the widow's mite, the rich young ruler, the man who needed larger barns, advice about paying taxes.[9] Some people choose to regulate their spending by giving a tenth (a tithe) to a person or organization of their own choosing, while others give money away on a larger scale. The stories that Jesus told have as much to say about what we have left as what we spend.

When I was a student, one of my friends used to come into class delighted every time she got a bargain. Bargains are great, but only if they are things we need: otherwise they are wasteful. Our enthusiasm for finding bargains embodies a deep yearning of the human spirit to receive something we neither deserve nor work for – what might be called 'grace' in a different context.

STRESS

This is one of the characteristics of modern living. Our forebears needed the rush of adrenalin to enable them to be good hunters and invigorate them to run from danger. Stress has the same effect, but nowadays we have few appropriate outlets for the pent-up energy. If you are painfully and continuously stressed, then you need to seek professional help, but anyone can benefit from bathing rituals or relaxation techniques. Create a routine of the things that work for you and spoil yourself a little. Massage has therapeutic mental, physical and spiritual benefits. If two people take time to learn how to do this properly they can work with each other to relieve physical stress, and in the process they will share their concerns, relieving their emotional stress, and provide that all important affirming physical contact with another person which is so hard to find in today's world.

Worry does not empty tomorrow of its sorrow. It empties today of its strength.
> *Corrie Ten Boom, Dutch survivor of Nazi death camp*
> *(1892–1983)*

Text Messages

This is the ideal way to convey wisdom to one another throughout the day, to build relationships and to show you care, whether someone is facing major trauma or just having a 'bad hair day'. Like emails, text messaging transcends the generations. I text my two daughters-in-law regularly, and I can testify that it helps us build our family community although we live a day's journey from one another. We do need to work at engaging across the generations, and this is one of those instances where I think those who are older and have more life experience should take a lead by making the effort and acquiring new skills.

Visitors

The care with which we welcome guests will either nurture friendship or leave them wondering if they have arrived at the

wrong time. It is not the expense that counts, but the consideration. Think about what will give this particular guest pleasure:
books, towels, paper tissues, toiletries, writing materials, clean
bedding, favourite foods, the availability of telephone, TV or
computer. In other words, loving your neighbour as you love
yourself.[10]

WORK

We spend a lot of time in our places of work, so take time to
create a holistic environment. Choose tools or equipment that are
specific to your occupation and have your name fixed on them.
Make or buy a suitable container for your personal items.
Whether your workspace is a workshop, office, desk, or just a
notice board, use personal things to help integrate it with the rest
of your life. Display photographs of your partner, children and
pets; frame a motto that you find inspirational to encourage you
when the going gets tough. Use fresh flowers to brighten up dark
corners. When you find yourself constantly working late, consider this to be an invitation to take stock of life. Reflect
periodically on why you do what you do. When we regard our
daily work as something of spiritual value, this will translate into
our work performance and the value we place on it, and ultimately on ourselves. As well as providing for ourselves and
those we support, work also allows us to develop our talents and
gives us opportunities to contribute to the wider community.
When it is safe and practical, those working late or on the night
shift might take time to light a candle and think of those who
are at home, at that moment placing them in the care of their
spiritual guardian. If you have to sign in or out of work, why not
allow this apparently mundane action to be a moment of dedica-
tion to give of your best and invite the Creator of all things to
enable you to bring grace into the lives of those with whom you
work. 'Grace' in this context might include treating one another
as persons rather than numbers – and we all know the difference
that can make.

In today's market place many of us make the mistake of concentrating on what we do rather than who we are or are becoming. Society encourages us to introduce ourselves to others by reference to their jobs, sometimes prefixing it with 'I'm only a ...'. Doing this reveals two things about ourselves: that we do not think we are important, and we do not think what we do is of much value. The reality is the exact opposite: it is not what we do, but how we do it, that is important. The cash value society places on different jobs may bear no relationship to their true worth. Women who stay at home to raise their children often describe themselves as 'just a housewife', a sure sign that they feel undervalued because they are not paid a financial reward. The reality is that time invested in rearing children and the holistic nurture of persons within a family makes an enormous contribution to the stability and well-being of every society. Similarly with jobs that are poorly paid or require little training: nobody wants to do them, yet these tasks are the essential building blocks of any economy. The starting point for any work-related ritual will be the need to recognize that all our work is valuable, and to identify helpful ways of honouring this for ourselves.

CHAPTER FIVE

FEASTS
AND
FESTIVALS

1: ADVENT

This is a time of preparation for Christmas and the coming of the
Christ child. In our consumer culture it is one of the most stressful times of year, so it is especially important to choose your
own rituals rather than allowing the activities to choose you.
Advent ('coming') is about love entering the world in the form
of a vulnerable baby – one reason why 'Christmas is for the
children' – so enable your children to discover the joy of
simplicity by creating gifts for family and friends.

THE ADVENT CALENDAR

One of my favourites to buy is a candle with the numbers one to
twenty-four down the side, which can be burned down one number each day at meal times, accompanied by reading aspects of
the Christmas story. When my children were young, I made a
calendar from a large sheet of fabric with 24 pockets stitched
onto it, and decorated with Christmas designs. The pockets contain a small gift for each of the days in Advent – and when the
season is finished, it can be stored away for another year.
Bringing this out and filling its pockets has become an annual
ritual in itself.

The Advent Crown

A circle of greenery is constructed, with four candles spaced evenly for use on each Sunday in advent, and a fifth candle in the centre for Christmas Day. Beginning with one candle lit on the first Sunday of Advent, an additional one is illuminated on each of the following Sundays, so that the light gets brighter towards Christmas Day as our expectations heighten.

Christmas Cards

Friends and colleagues around the world still keep in touch through this annual ritual. Instead of reading them when they are delivered, place the cards in a basket and then open them after your main meal. Each person can open a card in turn and read the greeting. It provides an opportunity to share with children the 'story' of these people – who they are, where we met them – and in the process passes on something of our family history. Such stories remind us all of key events in our lives and the import- ance of friends and community. Why not choose a favourite card each year and add it to your permanent collection of family mementoes?

It is good to be children sometimes, and never better than at Christmas, when its mighty Founder was a child Himself.

Charles Dickens, English novelist (1812–70)

Christmas Crackers

These can be expensive and contain very little, which is why we began making our own. Collect empty toilet tissue rolls, buy the strips that make the bang from a craft store, and cover them with decorative paper on the outside. This was one of my son's regular rituals as a teenager, and he still continues the tradition in his own home for a new generation.

Christmas Trees

Depending on where you live, think of collecting a tree from the forest where it grew. In any case, make a ritual of going and choosing, taking others who live with you, and then preparing it for its special place. This has become the source of well-repeated stories in my own family: the struggles of securing it onto the car, the day we bought one that was too big for the house door, the time we scuffed the paintwork or knocked pictures off the walls – not to mention trying to make old Christmas tree lights work for a new season (a ritual in itself, and always resolved more easily before the lights go on the tree).

Decorations

I still have some from my own childhood. They are no longer the most beautiful, but each has its own story. Others have been made by my children over the years, but I always add one or two new ones each year, symbolizing growth alongside history. One of my favourites is a fir cone sprayed with gold paint and wrapped up in a ribbon with the inscription, 'As this cone opened in the sunshine may you open up to God's love this Christmas'. It came from a church where I was guest preacher at an advent service, and the children made one for each person there.

Once everyone is asleep I love to sit quietly illuminated only by the lights on the tree, and reflect on the dawning of Christmas and what it will mean this year for me, for my family, my friends – and people all around the world. It offers me a space to reflect on where I fit into it all. You can also create an opportunity for children to sit with you and enjoy the colour of the tree and lights, and to nurture their spirit by telling the Christmas story.

Lanterns

This is a north European custom, to guide the Christ child to the door. You can use glass paints to decorate empty jars for this purpose, and then drop tea lights into them. In my part of the world, it can be dark by three in the afternoon at Advent, and I have often lit a little lantern with a candle and placed it in the window to welcome visitors and encourage passers-by.

Plum Puddings and Christmas Cake

Home baking is almost a thing of the past, but I still aspire to make puddings and Christmas cake. It is a wonderfully messy and fun way to spend an entire day – and accessible for all ages. This was a special ritual for my husband's grandmother, who was physically handicapped from her late teens, and had difficulty in walking as well as being unable to use one hand. But she was always included in this preparation for Christmas, and with her apron on would stay at the kitchen table for much of the day, using her 'good' hand to mix the puddings and cake, stirring in her wishes for those who would in due course consume the finished products. Not only was this a life-giving ritual for her, but the recounting of the story has itself become a ritual!

Yule Log

A yule log is a cake shaped like a log, covered in chocolate icing and marked with a fork to resemble the bark of a tree, then sprinkled with icing sugar to suggest the appearance of snow. One elderly man told me his family always had one that was cut and eaten when they returned home from a midnight church service on Christmas Eve. Such rituals are especially valuable nowadays, when our work and other responsibilities take family members to so many different places throughout the year, as they draw us back to our roots, and reaffirm our connections with place and people on whom we can depend for support and affirmation, in bad times as well as good.

Cleaning the Brasses

As a child, I remember polishing a big Indian brass bell so it would be bright and shining for Christmas, and then as an adult I started to acquire candlesticks and other metal bits and pieces that somehow always looked at their dullest by December. One day a friend with children of a similar age to mine asked me, 'Do you clean brass and silver for Christmas?' 'Yes,' I replied. 'Then why don't we spend a morning at each other's house', she proposed: 'I'll help you and then you help me, it will be much more fun.' She was right, and it actually became a ritual throughout the time I lived near her. Work became a pleasure as we talked and shared together – and the silver and brass shone to welcome Christmas.

If someone said on Christmas Eve,
  Come see the oxen kneel ...
I should go with him in the gloom,
    hoping it might be so.
     Thomas Hardy, English poet & novelist (1840–1928)

Christmas Day

Most families have favourite rituals for Christmas Day. As an antidote to sophistication, I always like to include something small and ordinary in children's presents. One is a pot of bubbles, and if they are produced at bedtime you can use them to give thanks for all the happenings of the day. Blow a stream of bubbles, and then mention out loud all the good things that have happened – or, as is often the case at holiday times, all the not-so-good things. As the bubbles disappear, use a refrain such as, 'As the bubbles rise and burst, we know our prayers are heard.'

People of all ages can enjoy this, and if everyone takes part it can be a way of celebrating family identity and solidarity.

Dancing Christmas Carols

This is another thing that is appropriate for all ages. You can clear the floor and do it in your own home, or hire a local venue and invite friends and neighbours. Carols were originally songs that were danced to, and over the years we kept the words and lost the dance. This means that simple steps can be used with most traditional Christmas songs. It needs some advance thought and planning, of course, to organize the music (tapes or CDs can be just as effective as a live band), and get some idea of the sort of movements that might work well with particular pieces. Give clear instructions for the dancing, but remember it's a party and don't be too bossy, and if younger children will be there, think through what will work for them. Depending on the weather where you live, you could start it off by singing carols at different homes, picking up the people on the way. Create breaks by having a musical item or story in between the dances. And some food will be welcome (and can be shared) – though not too much of it, as at this time of year many people have more than they can eat anyway.

2: Lent

This is a period of forty days prior to Easter in which Christians reflect on Christ's suffering and consider their own lifestyle. It was originally a time of fasting, but people today are more likely to give up some favourite food or drink, or some favourite activity. Others feel that a more appropriate spiritual discipline is to be intentional about doing something, rather than giving things up. One man I know tells me that sometimes he just sits in total silence for thirty minutes each day in the midst of his hectic life. One night he went out and had his half hour gazing at the stars and actually seeing them, while another day he went to the beach, watching the waves crashing on the shore and the weather clouds changing.

Ash Wednesday

This day signals the beginning of Lent. In most churches there is a ritual in which crosses are painted on the foreheads of worshippers, using ash made by burning palm crosses from the previous year's Palm Sunday celebration, and thereby signifying our identification with Jesus' suffering. You could also do this informally with friends. Take a few moments to meditate on what it would mean for you to take up your cross and follow Jesus, and then mark a cross on one another's heads, hands or feet. What does this symbolize for you? Seal by holding hands and saying, for example, 'Today I take the mark of the cross on my palms, a sign that I want to serve my fellow human beings as Christ did.' You could wash it off, but leaving it to fade naturally will give you a space to consider how you will keep this promise.

Maundy Thursday

This marks the last time that Jesus met to eat with his disciples before he was crucified. At this meal Jesus took some of the items that were on the table – bread and wine – and gave them new meaning. He knew what was ahead and recognized that in the immediate aftermath of his death his friends would be confused. So he took time to offer them hope for the future – by creating a new ritual. Today this ritual is celebrated by Christians in many different ways and with many different names: Holy Communion, Lord's Supper, Eucharist, Mass, Breaking of Bread. It can be very meaningful in a grand ceremony, but the simplicity of it can also be created wherever you are, using (as Jesus did) common food and drink, appropriate to your own culture.

Designate a sacred space and sit around it with your

friends, either on the floor or on chairs if that suits you better. Lay out a cloth or use a small table, with the food and drink you will use. Then read the story from the Bible.[1] At this supper Jesus also took a bowl of water and a towel and started to wash his disciples' feet.[2] In Palestine this was an everyday custom: feet got dusty from wearing sandals and it was considered a common courtesy for the servant to wash the guests' feet on arrival at the master's house.[3] By this action Jesus, the host at the dinner, was demonstrating the nature of true friendship and gave his disciples a model for how they should behave to one another. Jesus' friend Peter was not having any of this, and considered it would be improper for his leader to wash his feet. Then when Jesus insisted, he responded with, 'Oh well wash the whole lot – my head, my feet everything!' Such a character! But his impulsiveness highlights something important about the nature of commitment – to God and to one another.

You could do this in a group as a way of symbolically committing yourselves to supporting one another. One person doesn't need to do it for everyone: think laterally, and everyone has a turn. It is of course important to at least know the name of the person whose feet you are going to wash – and dry. Put a fragrance in the water like lavender, using enough so that it pervades the whole room. Have some relevant music playing in the background while you do this. This will create an appropriate environment in which to turn to the food and drink. Give thanks for the bread, break it and as you pass it to each other say, 'Christ provides this bread to nourish you'. Take the wine and as you share it say, 'Christ invites you to become a whole person'. This kind of Agape ('love') Feast was common in the early church.

GOOD FRIDAY

This is the day when Jesus was crucified. It is impossible to mark it effectively without reading the story, either on your own or with a group in your home or in church. The place is not crucial in that sense, but setting the atmosphere is. In churches with elaborate altars, the fine cloths are stripped away: perhaps removing all the extra clutter from your room would be a good place to start if meeting more informally with a group of friends. As well as a Bible from which to read the story, you will also need music, incense, a sturdy branch from a tree, some large nails, a hammer, a bowl of water, a candle and matches.

Begin with quiet music, then read the story.[4] Have a time of silence for folk to reflect on what Jesus' death might mean for them. People may choose to use water as a sign of cleansing, or to hammer a nail into the branch as a symbol that they wish to be identified with Christ, leaving behind the pain they have accumulated in life. When people have had sufficient time to respond to these things, play some music softly, light the incense and a candle as a sign of hope. You could also make a crown of thorns either in advance or as a corporate activity – use branches which will bend easily (pieces of bramble or briar work well). Alternatively, barbed wire can be used, with care, in the same way. Pass the crown of thorns round from hand to hand, as people reflect on it. It is probably best to leave people free to leave the room and regroup in another room when they are ready. Some people will need longer than others. In some churches there is a tradition of lighting a series of candles before the story of the crucifixion is read, and then at each significant point in the story a candle is extinguished until the place is in total darkness – as it was on the original Good Friday, according to the Bible story.

Friday–Saturday

I am placing this ritual in here but it could equally well be done on Friday, Saturday or Sunday. It requires as large a canvas as you can provide – if you have a group then it needs to be at least 3.4 x 2.8 metres. You could use new material or an old sheet. After reading the Easter story, give people disposable gloves to wear, supply a selection of different colours of paint, and invite them to paint their response to the story on the canvas and then return to you. Take the glove off, turning it inside out and leaving their hand clean and as you do so say, 'You are stained no more' – words which draw attention to Christ's suffering as a way of recreating us as whole people.

EASTER DAY

This is the day of resurrection, when some of Jesus' friends got the shock of their lives as they found the stone rolled away from the cave of burial and two angels announcing that Christ had risen. It has become a ritual in many countries to climb to the top of a hill where the sunrise can be seen. Climbing in the dark requires good organization with torches and – in cold climates – warm clothes and something warm to drink. But it does create a sense of pilgrimage that encapsulates the dark hours before resurrection. It's worth doing this at least once in a lifetime – but you will find it readily becomes a ritual. Sit in the silence at the top of the hill and watch the sun rise, choose music to sing or play to greet this special day. If you can take a trumpet and someone to play it, this is an appropriate instrument to honour the occasion. Several times I have danced in hiking boots on the top of a Scottish hill on a misty Easter morning and seen the assembled company gasp as the mist parted and the sun shone through while we danced to greet the risen Christ. Descending the mountain is such a contrast in the daylight, especially in the northern hemisphere where resurrection day coincides with the new life of nature after the darkness of winter. But wherever you are, it is a symbolic reminder of resurrection bringing light and hope into the darkest areas of life. This is the light worth carrying with you each day of your spiritual journey. Of course, plan to share breakfast with friends: you will need it after your climb, and will be in no hurry to separate anyway. Have the breakfast table decorated with bunches of yellow flowers (daffodils will be plentiful at this time of year in the northern hemisphere).

Alternatively (or in addition), why not have a champagne breakfast to celebrate this special day, to share food with friends and to tell the Easter story. Then there are Easter eggs, tradition-ally hard-boiled eggs that were decorated and rolled down a hill on this day (symbolic of the stone being rolled away from the tomb). This is still a fun thing to do, especially with friends. Simnel cake is another traditional Easter food: a rich fruit cake with marzipan through the centre. Children can make cakes safely using a no-bake recipe, shaping the mixture like a birds' nest and placing little speckled chocolate 'eggs' in the centre.

Then there is the Easter garden. Making this can be a good project for children on holiday from school. Choose a large flat tray or piece of wood, cover it with moss and use clay or some-thing similar to make a hill to represent the cave where Jesus' body was placed. Choose a stone to be rolled away to the side. In tiny jars or egg cups place some water and small fresh seasonal flowers. Cover the pots with moss so the flowers look as though they were growing in your Easter garden – and use it not just to display the story, but also to tell it.

Do not abandon yourselves to despair.
We are the Easter people and hallelujah
is our song.

Pope John Paul II (1920–2005)

3: Other Christian Festivals

Pentecost

This is the church's birthday, and comes fifty days after Easter.[5] After the resurrection Jesus kept surprising his friends by just turning up when they were least expecting him. One time it was to a group who were hiding in an upstairs room,[6] afraid that they might meet the same end as their friend. On another occasion he cooked breakfast on the beach to greet them as they landed their boats after fishing.[7] I recently went to a 50th birthday party in New Zealand. It was a warm sunny evening, and the birthday boy was an artist – on the grand scale. Just for the night, one part of the garden had been turned into a beach and water area so the children could play. Then as I moved through the garden to sit down, I noticed a sculpture, an iron cross made from railway tracks with upturned wine bottles attached all over it and water pumping up through the cross and spilling out in an abundance of grace. As the night sky rolled over, another sculpture which looked like a tree suddenly started to glow and burn. Each branch had a clump of volcanic rock at the end which was soaked in kerosene, so that when it was lit it burned but was not extinguished. I don't know whether to recommend this for Pentecost – but it certainly reflected the spirit of that occasion, when something like tongues of fire descended on the disciples and changed them forever.

All Saints Day (November 1st)

In the Christian calendar, this is a day for connecting with the transcendent dimension of life, recalling those who have passed on, including especially those who have made a memorable contribution to the life of their nations and communities. You could discover about a new saint each year. Create a journal of your findings, including a picture. Identify the people you would nominate as saints. Add a photograph to your journal of those who have helped, supported, or influenced you – whether of worldwide fame or very personal acquaintance. Try to identify the wisdom you have gained from each person and record your findings.

4: Seasons and Celebrations

All countries have their own national holidays, some of them connected to the seasons of the year (American Thanksgiving) while others celebrate traditional heroes (St George's Day in England, St Patrick's Day in Ireland, St Andrew's Day in

Scotland and St David's Day in Wales). Others take their origins from significant historical events (American Independence Day, Armistice Day in Britain, Anzac Day in Australia and New Zealand). Many of these events have their own specific traditions, and all of them reflect significant aspects of the culture of those countries. When we celebrate our culture it links us to our own roots, but is also an opportunity to introduce friends and neighbours from other cultures to our celebrations and then in turn to join their feasts, bringing us closer in understanding to each other. In this section, I have gathered together some typical occasions that fall into this category.

ALL FOOLS DAY (APRIL 1ST)

According to one ancient account, this day originated with Jesus, who 'tricked the devil' by rising from the dead. But the kind of tricks we now associate with this day stem from a tradition in the medieval church, when ordinary priests had a holiday with permission to poke fun at their leaders. This eventually got out of hand and was banned, but the tradition of the Holy Fool continues and today's Christian clowns take some of their inspiration from these jesters. Clowns are the masters at showing us our own foolishness. A joke is good when it helps us to laugh at ourselves and see our pomposity, cutting us down to size if we have grown too big for our boots. The ritual itself is giving a gift to each of your families and friends which enables them to laugh at least one day in the year. Laughter is a great medicine, and All Fools Day can be wonderful therapy for us if tricks are done in this way. Problems start when pranksters deliberately try to annihilate their victim, so before doing something pause to ask yourself how you would feel about having it done to you. 'First get rid of the log from your own eye; then perhaps you will see well enough to deal with the speck in your friend's eye'.[8]

Harvest and Thanksgiving

Harvest is a season rather than a date, though in the USA its celebration is marked by a national holiday on the fourth Thursday of November. The origins of the American festival go back to 1621, when the first harvest was reaped by the Pilgrims whose colony at Plimouth Plantation laid the foundations for the modern USA. Nowadays, much of the celebration has been taken over by merchandise and marketing, but for those who want to be thankful for the good things in life this still provides a wonderful annual focus – and the need to give thanks is, after all, common to all races and peoples. One of the paradoxes of life today is the contrast between our ability to communicate around the globe more or less instantaneously and our evident inability to create meaningful community in our own backyards. One of the things I like best about American Thanksgiving is that it is also a homecoming, when families commit themselves to be together. This is something that we could all learn from, especially now that family members may live in different countries, and be connected to several families through marriage and remarriage. Most of us have to choose who to include as family on any given occasion, but it is still worth making the effort – and for those with no contact with their birth family, there is always the opportunity to meet with others whom we consider to be our community.

Food will always be part of any celebration linked to harvest. It can be simple. In the US, turkey and pumpkin pie is the traditional fare. Here is an idea for celebrating harvest, which could be used anywhere. How about a cheese and wine party with a difference? Decorate the room with harvest fruits, fir cones, and autumn flowers and branches. Choose harvest themes for napkins and tableware. But on this occasion, remove the labels from the wine bottles before your guests arrive, and display them somewhere. Number the bottles and invite the guests to taste each wine and guess which label goes with it. Do the same with cheeses. Invite each guest to bring a harvest offering, possibly one they have made or grown, (or bought if this is not practical for them). During the evening each person tells why it is particularly significant to them (maybe it reminds them of berry picking with their family, or whatever). Include any sort of goods (not just food), and depending on your situation it may be that you would want to donate them later to some charity, or individuals known to you. As part of this, each person could say what they have been most thankful for in the given year. You might also make in advance an outline of each person on paper (it does not have to be too accurate), stick them around the room, supply papers, magazines and pens and then invite people to choose pictures or write comments on the figures to tell what they appreciate about each person. It will be surprising and affirming to see each others' perceptions. You will be able to take this home and enjoy it for the rest of the year – at least.

Sharing food on an even more regular basis is a custom that still lingers in some rural areas, notably in New England where it would be possible to have a bean supper in a different community venue every week of the year. A similar idea still survives in the north of England with the tradition of pie and pea or potluck suppers. Everyone brings from the bounty of their store cupboard and shares with everyone else.

If the only prayer you said in your whole life was 'thank you', that would suffice.
Meister Eckhart, German Christian mystic (1260–1327)

Halloween (October 31st)

I have included this here because it is loosely associated with harvest, both in its timing and the themes with which it is celebrated worldwide. In recent years, some Christians (especially in Britain) have claimed there is a problem because of its pagan origins – though in truth, the timing of all our traditional Christian festivals goes back to the same roots! In any case, it seems to me that the significance of a ritual is not intrinsic to what we do but depends on the meaning we invest in it. This is certainly a case where the American tradition can point us in new directions, with its clear connection between Halloween and harvest made not only through the ever-present pumpkins, but also the scarecrows which, having done their job for the season, would traditionally be brought in from the fields along with the crops they had protected. The cheery faces of carefully crafted pumpkin lanterns can bring light on to our paths, and invite us to have a party and some fun as the dark days of winter begin to draw in. I remember in Scotland as a child enjoying church parties at which all the traditional Halloween games were played: the treacle scone which hung on a string and was almost impossible to bite without getting a face full of treacle, because of course someone was swinging the string; ducking in a tub of water for apples; and dressing up. Children love to dress up, and adults love the excuse to do so: for many who have lost touch with their inner child this is an opportunity to play and rediscover themselves in a safe environment. This is a festival that is a natural time for storytelling, whether the stories are traditional folk tales or our own family history. With so many possibilities, you don't need an excuse for a party: just get on and make your own, with your own rituals.

Bonfire Night (November 5th)

This is a distinctively English celebration, marking the day in 1605 when Guy Fawkes planned to blow up the Houses of Parliament in London. His plot was discovered, he was tortured and executed, and this macabre tale is still told and celebrated with annual bonfires, most of which are topped with effigies of Guy himself and nowadays usually accompanied by a firework display.[9] The making of 'the guy' and of the bonfire itself were traditionally community endeavours occupying weeks in the life of a typical village, though nowadays many bonfires are organized on a semi-commercial basis and include outdoor barbecues (even though November is almost mid-winter in Britain). How is this a ritual? Well, it creates community and is a lot of fun. Moreover, the handing on of our historical stories to children is an important principle: this is where they discover their roots. The origin of bonfire night is definitely not a 'good' story: not only did the plotters intend to kill the monarch, but later generations often added an effigy of the pope to the fire, along with a guy (reflecting other religious tensions of the day). But it's important to tell the good and the bad stories of history so that our children can hopefully learn from the mistakes of their forebears. This story has the ability to underline the need for tolerance rather than violence, and promote negotiation over bullying – all important values in today's multicultural society.

Hogmanay (New Year's Eve)

This could just as easily have gone into the chapter on Beginnings and Endings, but it is a national celebration that is unique to Scotland (even the word 'hogmanay' is not recognized in other cultures). Earlier I mentioned our roots and our stories as being intrinsic to our identity, and so I share mine. In Scotland, there are many rituals traditionally connected with Hogmanay: putting out the ashes from the coal fire, cleaning the house, painting and decorating the house, taking a bath – all things that simply had to be done before the clock struck midnight. The details might vary, but these are all good things with which to create end of year rituals. As you do the mundane jobs, you have time to reflect and to consider changes that have occurred in past months – and the changes you aspire to in the coming year. You could include clearing the desk, the loft, the shed, the garage and probably the car too.

Some people in Scotland will go out to a ceilidh (traditionally, dancing and storytelling), while others will wait for the 'first foot' to arrive and hope it will be a tall, dark, handsome male, heralding good fortune for the New Year. Whatever you do, give yourself some time during this day to make your end of year assessment: you won't do it so well if you wait until the festivities are over. We usually keep our Christmas cake to cut at midnight: it lets us enjoy the decoration longer and saves over-indulging prematurely. It also solves the problem of what to eat – and there will always be enough for whoever comes by. Light a candle in the window to bring in the New Year. Have your resolutions prepared. Take a moment's silence to usher out the old year and listen at the gate of the new. Think of all the possibilities. If you are the one who takes the lead in your house, you might give each member a new journal to encourage them to be intentional in their reflections throughout the coming year. Choose books appropriate to the recipient: an artist's sketch book to an artist, a scrap-book to a child, a grandparents' book to a new grandparent. Think of making books from handmade paper – or at least wrapping ordinary books in handmade paper – and decorating to suit the recipient. Include attractive writing utensils: pens, pencils, pastels, quills, paints, or crayons for children. Get people to share their New Year's resolutions. Invite everyone present to put their name in the signatures book.[10]

New Year's Day

Morning people will enjoy getting out and having a bracing walk, regardless of the weather. Enjoy the natural world and its beauty, take your camera and keep your eyes open for trophies, bits of wood, shells, or logs. If you're in the city, a walk will be every bit as interesting as if you're in the countryside: in most parts of the world, this day is a national holiday, and you will be surprised how different even urban streets look without the bustle of a working day. After a long walk it's warming to be greeted with a glass of mulled wine (in the northern hemisphere anyway: in the south you might need to be cooled down). Toast one another, absent friends and families, and have a combined effort to produce food for the day. Let each person bring something to the meal – not necessarily food, but other contributions such as creating place names or folding the napkins in a distinctive way. Many rituals are created around particular types of food that we identify with specific experiences or emotions. Ever since the year when I received a card telling me there was a surprise in the freezer, we have always had smoked salmon at some point in the festivities. This goes back to the days before smoked salmon was in every supermarket, and at the time I had never tasted it. So a gift of Scottish smoked salmon was special, and has become a ritual reminder of my husband's care for the mundane aspects of life, such as cooking food. Whatever you eat, linger over the meal and enjoy conversation: this is what you will need to sustain you in days to come. And if you haven't yet exchanged your reflections for the past year and aspirations for the New Year, now is a good time.

5: Making it Special

For some individuals, meeting new people can turn a special occasion into a daunting experience. I now usually take the initiative in such situations, hold my hand out to shake hands and say, 'Hello, I'm Olive'. It seems remarkably straightforward, but it is extraordinary how few people seem willing to take this kind of approach. Some people still don't know how to respond, but most times the other person is relieved that someone else has started the conversation.

Food is naturally at the centre of feasts and festivals, so place settings are important and can become a ritual if we are intentional in our action. Many of the ideas grouped together in this section can be used in connection with some of the specific occasions dealt with elsewhere, both in this chapter and in others.

● Choose a colour for the table that will reflect the occasion: red and green are popular at Christmas, while yellow reflects spring and therefore works well in a northern hemisphere Easter. Take time to set your table, and as you set the various items think of those who will be part of the celebration. Say their names and express what you wish for each of them individually or as a group. Fold the napkins in a particular way to suit the occasion or the person.

- Design the place names with the event in mind. Include a wise saying for each person. Whenever I eat at a Chinese restaurant, I enjoy the ritual of opening and reading the fortune cookies, and have occasionally adapted this at home by serving a wise saying wrapped in filo pastry and quickly baked – though if you are short of time, you can just slip the saying inside the packet of an individually wrapped after-dinner chocolate. At some point during the meal, you can invite people to share the wisdom that was chosen for them. Doing this can create space between courses, and allows time to enjoy conversation and create community, slowing the whole event down so that it can be savoured and relationships can be enriched.

- When hosting a meal in my home, I always start with the lighting of a central candle, signifying that we place those who are special to us in the Great Creator's care. I invite my guests to include their closest friends and others they may be thinking about. It is also a time to mention anyone who has a particular need of healing or support.

- The creating of effective rituals is often dependent on the attention to detail – and it is this forethought that can make the difference between something being just OK and becoming truly significant. Think about how many can comfortably be seated at a table. Will conversations be able to take place across the table as well as between those seated alongside each other? There is nothing worse than being at a large circular or rectangular table and finding yourself stuck between two conversations, unable to connect with anyone. When placing guests, make sure everyone has a companion to talk to, taking particular care of shy folk or those who are vulnerable (e.g. someone recently divorced or bereaved, or with another major life change in progress). Be careful about putting together people who know each other too well, as they may get caught up in their own private conversations and possibly exclude others – even with the best intentions. If you have a large number of people sitting down for a meal it is a good idea to have a ritual of changing places between each course. This ensures that any difficult pairings will not last all evening – and it's also fun. How often have you come away from an event feeling you've only been able to talk with half the folk?

- When I have a large group where buffet food is required for the numbers and the folk know each other well – like students who have studied together, or a group who work together – I might hand out pieces of matzo and invite people to break a piece off and give it to another, as they do so telling them something they appreciate about them or have valued in the workplace or have learned from them. People love being given permission to do this, and also value the affirmation they receive, particularly in British culture where there can be a tendency to be more outspoken in our criticisms than our commendations.

- Another ritual I have had at a large party where folk don't all know one another is to provide a variety of drinks with the food – nothing special there! – but to ask people not to fill their own glass. Instead, they are to have someone else fill their glass, and at the same time give them a wish or a blessing. This is a great way of getting folks mixing, because they think about each other and self consciousness fades as they build up relationships. There is always one person who is mindful of the cooks and finds their way to the kitchen to reward them!

The Little Door in Los Angeles is one of my favourite restaurants. It is literally a little door which you could easily miss in the street if you were unaware of its existence. Inside, though, both atmosphere and guest list give it the feel of a Hollywood party and you never know who might be sitting at the next table. But the more interesting thing to me is that before the proprietor opens for business each evening, he lights a smudge of sage leaves and moves through the restaurant blessing the staff and each table, and those who will eat there that night. This is a Native American cleansing ritual, and has a similar significance to the use of incense in the Christian tradition. I remember the first time I ate there. The fragrance of the smudge was still hovering in the air, and the server came to our table bearing a bowl of oil, a loaf of bread, and a bottle of wine. We all looked at each other, and saw new significance in our meal (incense, anointing, and sacrament). I have occasionally created a similar situation in my own home by sharing bread and wine in an intentional way between main course and dessert, in a similar way to what I have described above under Maundy Thursday. It is a wonderful opportunity to honour a special accomplishment, or to celebrate new opportunities, or indeed just to bless friends and family.

CHAPTER SIX

CHALLENGE AND CHANGE

It's not that some people have willpower and some don't - it's that some people are ready to change, and others are not.

James S. Gordon, American psychiatry professor

The way we react to the challenges of life determines who we become. Moments of change can drive us to the depths of despair or engender a greater vision and passion within us. Even difficult circumstances can become the catalyst for new possibilities and greater achievements by offering an opportunity to reassess our strengths and weaknesses and to understand more about ourselves. It can also happen the other way around, as what looks like a positive experience turns out to have negative consequences. And, of course, something that is stress-inducing for one person can be positively energizing for another. The one thing all such experiences have in common is the element of surprise. The unexpected can enable us to see things from a different perspective, not least by highlighting what is important and what is not. It offers a chance to refocus on the significant matters of life rather than the peripheral, and can bring us into contact with people, places, and experiences we might otherwise have chosen to avoid. Life can sometimes seem like an endless series of crisis points. The Chinese word for 'crisis' consists of two traditional characters, one meaning danger and the other meaning opportunity. Every testing occasion contains both elements: it is up to us to choose whether to focus on the danger or the opportunity. You might like to list all the experiences you can think of that have been particularly challenging in your life, putting them in two columns, positive and negative. You could find that you need a third column to express both elements within the same experience. For example, losing your job may at first be very negative, but if you then set up your own business and it proves to be successful you are likely to look back on the disruption as the 'best thing that ever happened'. This is one reason why keeping a journal and creating graphs[1] are both useful as ongoing disciplines: they enable us to reflect on and reassess the way life is going.

1: Stages of Life

Some key stages of life have already been covered in the chapter on beginnings and endings. Here we look at some other significant moments that we all live through.

The Driving Test

I still remember the excitement of getting my first full driving licence. Paradoxically, I was less apprehensive about driving then, with no experience, than I am now, with many years experience, especially when I drive in a country where traffic is on a different side of the road. It is important to know how to calm yourself for the test. So breathe deeply, imagine the examiner is not there, and drive the best you can. Refuse to be flustered by the unexpected. You can cope if you don't lose your head. If you fail, remember that you are not alone. Driving requires many skills to be integrated and coordinated – and you want to become a safe driver, not just to pass the test. Get someone to celebrate your progress so far, and plan how you are going to tackle stage two. Don't let it get you down: analyze what went wrong and plan to work on those things. Take more practice, and book yourself another test so you have a target to aim for.

If you pass, then congratulate yourself and invite someone to celebrate with you. Thank those who have supported you. When the successful candidate is a young person, their parents can have mixed feelings. Congratulations are certainly in order – along with a few ground rules if the newly qualified driver is to borrow the parent's car. The best ritual here is being single-minded enough to stick with whatever is agreed. Young people sometimes evolve their own ways of dealing with parental anxiety. The most zealous driver in my family was my second son, who chose to enrol for an advanced driving course and went on to pass that in a matter of months following his regular test. It was his way of demonstrating his capability – it certainly was a good idea – and he became a very responsible driver.

GETTING A PASSPORT

This used to be a very grown-up thing to have, but my grandson had one at only four months old. The occasion can be marked by framing the passport photo and sending copies to special people. It can also be the time to reflect on the places and people you might visit and, in these fearful days, of the big issues not only of safety and security but of justice for all the world's people. How can you bless those whom you will meet on your travels?

BLENDING FAMILIES

A blended family is one that is created when parents enter a new relationship and bring their children from previous relationships. The daily life of such families will be significantly shaped by the way the various children relate to one another. The transition will always be more challenging to children than adults, and they should be as fully included in the entire process as is possible. Children often provide significant stability to a divorced parent, and when that parent meets a new partner they can suddenly experience marginalization and a feeling of being robbed of a relationship they have in many respects sustained. The children of both parents are bound to be apprehensive about each other, and may harbour deep hostility to either or both adults as well as to their new adoptive siblings. Everyone in the blended family has several new relationships to deal with.

When a wedding creates a blended family, any of the ideas in chapter 2 could be incorporated and as well as the bride and groom exchanging rings, each child could receive some token gift (maybe even a ring, depending on their ages and preferences) that says 'You are important in this new family – in fact, you are a full founding member of it'. It might also be worth including some specific promises that are for the whole family – such as:

- doing tasks together
- listening to each other's music
- reading each other's books
- watching each other's films or TV programmes
- sharing skills – showing one another how to do new things
- eating together on a regular basis
- generally encouraging, challenging, and supporting one another

In all such circumstances, there will need to be a high degree of intentionality and a conscious commitment to invest time with one another in order to make this a reality.

Home Alone

Sooner or later the time comes for children to be left in the house by themselves. This is always stressful for any parent, because it evokes underlying issues of control and safety. It is crucial to establish some boundaries in advance, but not too many – so work out what is really important: matters of safety including no matches; not opening the door; how to answer the telephone. Once such things are agreed, there needs to be an element of trust on both sides and a very simple ritual can acknowledge this. It could be the handing over of a symbol such as a key, with some simple words exchanged along the lines of 'now you are in charge and I trust you', with the response, 'I accept the responsibility and I feel honoured that you believe in me.' Then the hardest part of all – you just have to trust, and pray. Or maybe send a text message while you're out of the house. Or if you are like me, you will end up doing all of these things!

GOING TO BED WHEN YOUR TEENAGE CHILD IS OUT

When your children become teenagers the foundations you have laid will be put to the test. Children with a strong sense of what is right and wrong will not easily reject the values they have learned, but remember that giving them the skills to say 'no' is not something that can be taught in five minutes before they leave for a party. But you can make sure they have a way out of awkward situations, and the mobile phone is a huge help here as teenagers will respond to a text message quite differently from how they would receive a regular phone call from you asking how they are getting on, or if they want a ride home. But the time will come when they will be out and you will be ready for bed. How about a lantern to light at the door (it's safe if you leave it outside) and when they get home they can turn it off and bring it inside. Then when you get up in the morning (or in the middle of the night!) you will have a sign that tells you they are home without needing to disturb them. For those who still feel anxious, before you go to bed pray for their protection, for the courage to do what they know is right and not to succumb to peer pressure. You might want to do this in your child's own room.

HEALTH SCARES

We all have days when we feel 'not quite right'. Allow yourself some rest, and pamper yourself, as well as taking appropriate medication. This is a good time to review your lifestyle and eating habits, and if you have to take time out then find something creative to do – sorting out photographs, completing a piece of work that has been put to one side. Read things that have been piling up that you would like to read. Watch some comedy on TV: humour is a great healer in itself.

With more serious ailments, find one or two people who will support you and pray with you. Write down your greatest fears and put them in a 'worry box' and leave the worry there, symbolically acknowledging that you have left your problem with a higher authority. Recent medical research has shown that prayer makes a difference when we face health problems, so if you haven't done this before perhaps now is the time to try. Native South American culture has a fascinating ritual for children: a coloured belt with a little string of dolls to each of which the child can talk in turn, sharing whatever is worrying them. This enables children to talk about their problems and then they too can be encouraged that, having voiced their problems, they can leave them in the hands of the Creator.

Poor health always invites us to consider deep questions about life, who we are, and what it all means. Our view of illness has been coloured by the biomedical model of health, which tends to identify well-being with bodies that are working like well-oiled machines. But it is perfectly possible to have a fully-functioning body and not be a whole person – and *vice versa*. Illness can be a place of growth and wisdom. That does not mean it will always be easy, and you may want to seek out a mentor to help you through a support group, local church or prayer group.

One of the secrets of life is to make
stepping stones out of stumbling blocks.

> Jack Penn, South African surgeon (1909–96)

WRITING A WILL

We should all do it. It offers an occasion to give thanks for all the
benefits you have received in living. Take legal advice so that
your wishes can actually be fulfilled, and not be thwarted by
some loophole in the law that you were unaware of. Write notes
to people telling them why you want them to have particular
items, and don't attach unnecessary conditions to your generosity. This is especially important when leaving money for
organizations: by including your own particular whims you can
often prevent anything happening in the future, simply because
some change has occurred in the situation which could not have
been anticipated. Giving requires that we relinquish the need to
control. This will not only free the recipient, but in so doing you
will free yourself and create a space to concentrate on your
spiritual development. Don't forget to name the person/s to
receive your journal. Things that you think are trivial could well
be treasured after you are gone. Most people whose diaries are
published never imagined they were writing anything of
significance to anyone other than themselves.

BECOMING A GRANDPARENT

Most adults know the temptation of wanting to live our lives
again through our children and grandchildren, and as the
rearrangement of families becomes ever more commonplace –
and complex — this is an ever-present challenge. Not everyone
has prior experience of their own grandparents, so there may not
be obvious role models. But that need not prevent the creation of
good relationships if you are intentional about it. Obviously if
you have a good relationship with your child and have worked at

developing relationships with their partner, you will have prepared the ground well. If rituals have been part of your life, then you might like to talk in advance about what the new parents think would be good rituals for grandparents to initiate and carry through. By all means suggest some, though the parents themselves might come up with some new and imaginative ideas, as well as dislike some of yours. Grandparents should also reflect on what kind of grandparents they want to be. What do you want to offer your grandchild? Gifts and money won't be the most important things, though grandparents are sometimes in a position to offer things at this stage in their life which they could not afford for their own children. But if grandparenthood focuses only on providing expensive toys or clothes, something very important has been lost. Keeping a journal of your relationship would be a good non-intrusive way to nurture a relationship over a period of time, while writing your own story to pass onto your grandchildren would be a lasting gift.[2] Writing regular letters and emails, or making phone calls, are good starting points, which can easily become a two-way process as your grandchild grows up and gains new skills. Craftwork can form a bond, and provide home-spun gifts for children to give to their parents and others, while grandparents taking kids to sports events, galleries, the cinema, and so on, can make life easier for the parents. Note, though, that the best help for hard-pressed parents is not always provided by grandparents taking the children away from the home: sometimes parents would love nothing more than time to enjoy their children, which can be facilitated by offering to do mundane daily chores about the house. Never forget that there will likely be two sets of grandparents, and one of the best rituals might be to vow not to be in competition with each other. Grandparents have a particular role in listening, and those who are retired may find they have additional time to offer their grandchildren. In some families, that has become an essential component in regular childcare, either at times of family breakdown or through the financial constraints encountered by young parents who need full-time work but are unable to earn enough to afford a nursery.

2: RELATIONSHIPS

CARING FOR OTHER PEOPLE'S CHILDREN

In today's fragmented society, foster-caring is of particular importance. In preparing to receive a foster child, invest the same love and attention as you would for your own child. The fact that a child needs care tells its own story, and though support will be available from social service agencies, you will need considerable inner spiritual resources if you are to make a worthwhile difference for the short time you have this child.

When a baby arrives in a new home to be fostered, many of the rituals mentioned in chapter 2 will be relevant, especially if care is to be long-term. Even for a shorter period, some specific way of recognizing the relationship is still invaluable. In this situation, a daily symbol can be a good idea. If you care for babies on a regular basis, then keep a book which has a special page for each child, to include notes about them, a photo, and any particular memories or experiences associated with them. When they leave, write a prayer or motto for each child summing up what you have learned from them and expressing the potential you have seen in them.

For older children, choose a symbolic action together which appeals to them. It might be something as simple as lighting a candle at the dinner table and thinking of all the special people in our lives (allowing the child freedom to reflect on things but not necessarily to articulate matters that are too painful). Or each member of the family could write the names of as many people or pets as they wish on separate pieces of paper and then place them in a basket. Depending on how many there are, you can take one out at each meal time and think especially of that individual or pet (or if a lot have been put in the basket, each person could take one out, mention the name and then say something about them or think about them). This has the advantage of including everyone in the family on the same footing, an aspect of prayer which gives it a particular value because adults and children all come in at the same level, and no one has a head start.

When talking of prayer, remember that there are many ways of doing this. One technique I have found helpful (in large public gatherings as well as more home-based occasions) is the use of bubbles, which were briefly mentioned in chapter 5. These are natural for a child to be playing with, and reflect the way many people see their prayers: as things of incredible beauty that might soar to great heights, yet constantly existing on the edge between permanence and fragility. With a child, you can take turns at blowing the bubbles and saying a prayer – which might be as simple as, 'I'm thinking of mum in hospital', to which the response could be, 'As the bubbles fall to the ground and burst, we know that our prayers are heard.' The good thing about this is that it creates space to say absolutely anything at all to God, while the use of the bubbles not only gives a visual representation but can also (precisely because of the fun that is usually associated with blowing bubbles) defuse what might otherwise be angry or difficult situations.

One of the biggest challenges in foster-care situations is how to encourage your own children to interact positively with the short-term visitors – something that is particularly fraught with difficulty if the foster children have had a hard time and are inclined to see kids in a more 'normal' family as having had special advantages. Many things can help to overcome this situation, but from the perspective of intentional ritual one suggestion is for the children to work together on constructing a big collage depicting all the things they each like. They could choose to do a different letter of the alphabet each day, selecting one or two things each time, and by the time they have done this for 26 days they should know a lot about each other and in the process be on the way to working out how to live peacefully together, maybe becoming good friends. A by-product is that by naming things of significance, they have the opportunity to acknowledge their anger, and hopefully then be helped to deal with it in productive and positive ways.

Causing an Argument

Whoever is slow to anger has great understanding, but one who has a hasty temper exalts folly.

Proverbs 14:29

No one ever plans to do this: it just seems to happen, and we only realize our own part in it after the event. It is always healthy if we can take responsibility for our own behaviour rather than looking for excuses to absolve ourselves. However, it really does take two or more to sustain an argument, so no single individual need take on the guilt of everyone. What we can do is admit our own part, and apologize. Many adults go through life without ever mastering the art of doing this sincerely and without sulking. Parents can encourage children to apologize in a meaningful way and without humiliating them – and, of course, that will be much easier for them if they see adults modelling this behaviour. It also creates respect in relationships if we seek forgiveness when we make mistakes. But anger is a funny thing, and your apology may not always be accepted – in which case you just have to live with the knowledge that you have done all you could to resolve the situation. So don't give up too readily, but do know when to move on. Even in a situation where something is not your fault, you can still take the initiative in putting things right. Having a drink together is not such a bad idea: the old adage about having your 'feet under the table' as a sign of acceptance stemmed from the fact that if you allowed someone to sit at your table they were relaxed in your presence and would not burst in as your enemy to do you harm. Some people will be more likely to respond to a different kind of gesture, such as having their favourite food cooked – while flowers and chocolates are still very acceptable ways of apologizing, so long as they are not a substitute for a real apology. Instead of a whole bouquet, why not try a single flower? And for a longer-term reminder of forgiveness, why not do something together, like planting bulbs and watching over them till they come into bloom, thereby allowing the care and watering that takes place to be a reminder of the nurturing we all need in our relationships? At the end of it all, though, move on. Be kind to yourself: God forgives, so you can too.

WHEN OTHERS ARE LATE

If people are habitually late, say for a meeting, make a point of starting on time to give respect to those who have managed to be on time. If you regularly start late, eventually everyone will turn up late. Make it known that you will start on time and never allow the latecomer to make you feel obliged to go back over the ground they have missed. If they ask, tell them you will inform them later.

WHEN PEOPLE FAIL YOU

It is tough, but it happens, and here the golden rule needs to be, 'Do unto others as you would have done unto you.' Try to be forgiving, and take account of whether the failure was due to an accidental mistake, or whether it was intentional. Ponder what you would like the outcome to be. Is it worth talking it over with the person involved? They may have no idea how you feel. But notice the operative words here are 'how *you* feel': it is always better to express disappointment in this way, rather than by attributing blame to someone else. If it can be resolved, you have kept a friend. If things are so bad that you have to walk away from the situation, you may need help, but try to leave your anger behind, for that in itself will be destructive for you.

*For every minute you are angry, you lose
sixty seconds of happiness.*

> Ralph Waldo Emerson, American poet & philosopher
> (1803–82)

Acknowledging Friendship Ended

Sometimes you just have to accept that you will not be able to work with a particular individual because of a personality clash or fundamental difference of worldview. Though St Paul had a lot to say to Christians in Corinth about the need to forgive one another before partaking of the Lord's Supper, he himself never quite connected with Mark and his relative Barnabas.[3] From what we know, they were all good people, they just found it impossible to work together and so they chose to go their separate ways, but at the same time blessed each other in doing so. That approach requires a good deal of openness but it has the advantage of ensuring that there is neither unfinished business nor bad feelings that might flare up in the future. If you find yourself in this situation, identify a way of coming to an amicable agreement and choose a small token to exchange as a mark of your mutual respect. We all have both strengths and weaknesses, and refusing to recognize this can store up many problems, not least when pent-up anger is handed down to future generations who can then find themselves locked in conflict about issues that should have been laid to rest years (even centuries) before. Think of all the wars that have started in this way.

3: Coming and Going

Leaving the House

We all do this every day – maybe more than once – so a ritual needs to be short and simple, or you will skip it. If you work out a system of switching off appliances and locking doors in the same order each time, it will save the trauma of wondering whether you did something once you are out. Leave all the things you will need ready by the door so nothing is forgotten, and as a back-up place a list of things you must take with you on a note on the back of the door: there is nothing more frustrating than leaving without some vital documents or keys. As you set the house alarm, pause to bless the house and your pets. By observing this moment of transition you are less likely to bolt headlong into disaster. Take time to realize that one of life's finest qualities is the ability to be present in the moment: you have no guarantee of another.

Going on Holiday

This is a more extended form of everyday coming and going. Plan ahead to ensure that regular deliveries are cancelled in time, and to consider whether the appearance of your house, the presence or absence of mail deliveries, or of a car parked outside, will advertise the fact that you are away from home. Check with a trusted friend or neighbour to water plants and generally keep an eye on things for you. Though you're unlikely to need it, leave a contact number for emergencies and make sure your friend knows your email address. You will enjoy your holiday much better knowing that others can be in touch if they need to be. Remember that your spirit needs a holiday at least as much as your body and your mind. Take a book, sketchpad and paints, candles, or a note to remind you of the things you need for a given ritual – or just a promise to yourself to take time to meditate and enjoy the new environment. As you depart, bless the house and those you leave behind.

Going on a Long Journey

If you are getting into the habit of incorporating rituals into everyday life, then you will find it is like building a wall: the simple things you do each day are the first building blocks, and a longer or more intense event involves adding other blocks which have a particular significance for specific occasions. This in itself gives a sense of continuity as well as simplicity. When I go on a long trip, I always tidy my desk. It is one of the few times it is regularly well cleared, but I would not travel with peace of mind if I knew I had outstanding papers to deal with on my return. Once away from home, the sending of text messages and emails has become a ritual of travel for me. If schedules allow, I send emails or text messages to all my family, and it is the first thing I aim to do once I arrive safely in another country. It perhaps goes without saying that a long trip will always go more smoothly if we draw up lists in advance, planning our packing in relation to the different locations to be visited. Rituals for journeys need to be portable and compact, but remember to take some pictures with you: people you meet will always be interested to see your home, friends, and family.

Travel can affect our whole worldview as well as our self-understanding. I remember visiting Singapore for the first time, and finding my understanding of World War II transformed by the realization that the British forces were literally looking the other way when the Japanese invaded. In New Zealand, I recently met a woman who told me that when she first visited London she was enthralled just to touch the stones of Westminster Abbey and other ancient sites. It gave her a connection with the history she had read about, and also with her ancestors even though they had left Britain generations before. Many people find this sense of spiritual connection changes a holiday into a pilgrimage, especially when visiting locations filled with personal memories or connected with traditional stories or significant personalities.

Emigration

Deciding to emigrate is usually the end of a long process of significant changes in a person's life. It no longer has the finality that it did for previous generations, when those who moved to a new country were as good as dead to those who were left behind. But despite all the talk about globalization – and the fact that shops all over the world look increasingly similar, with the same goods on sale – you are still going to miss some things. Find out where you can buy your favourite foods from the home country, maybe even get your friends and relatives to send you a food parcel (though choose carefully, as exporting and importing food can create all sorts of unexpected complications). Though my home base is in Scotland, I am living overseas as I write this, and I have just made a pot of lentil soup (a traditional Scottish favourite). It is amazing how much better I feel for it: not just the taste, but the smell as it cooks, the familiarity of the process and the memories it recalls. Food can play a significant part in feeling at home: not only can you explore the traditional dishes of your new culture, but you can create new friendships by inviting others to experience the food and culture of your home country. Sharing food is the basis of community the world over, and though we all know a lot about different cultures through movies, or books, or TV programmes, encountering a real person creates a different dynamic. It quite literally is 'the way you do it' that makes it special. Sharing even a simple thing in this way will give you a new realization of who you are, an understanding of what makes you tick, and you will probably in turn have a new appreciation of your own culture, your roots and your connectedness.

Saying Goodbye

We say goodbye to other people many times in a day, and every day in life. It is important that we have simple rituals for doing so, and where possible we avoid rushing through them. None of us knows what life holds next. Every goodbye may be the last one: we may not get another opportunity, and that would be a much harder thing to address than a few moments apparently 'lost' in the midst of a busy schedule. I remember once when I had been visiting my son, and he accompanied me to catch the train to the airport. We had plenty of time, and I was enjoying these final moments in his company since I knew I would be unlikely to see him again for several months. Unexpectedly, an earlier train that had been delayed somewhere pulled up to the platform, and we both did what seemed obvious: eager to help me, he opened the door, I jumped on board, and the train was immediately on its way. As soon as I had done it, I realized it was a very unsettling ending to what had been a special visit. The unexpected speed of my departure meant that for me there was no closure on that occasion.

It is natural to want to do something special with a friend whom you will not see for a considerable time. Eating together is an obvious thing to do, though this is not the time to make that gourmet meal you have always wanted to share. Do that a few weeks in advance of the parting. When the time comes, keep it simple: you will be surprised how tense such an occasion can become! So work through in advance how you want that final meal or conversation to go. There is no harm in showing emotion so that others know the depth of your love for them, but be aware of the fact that the other person will be struggling with their own feelings. Exchange small tokens, maybe something significant for the journey or a little treasure to tuck in a pocket or to wear. It will be a constant source of pleasure in the future. Hold one another and trust yourselves into the care of God – who does care about such things. Friendship bracelets are a popular item which can be made and exchanged, or you might buy one of those pieces of jewellery which comes in two halves that fit together like a jigsaw but which each of you can wear separately. Those who are married will recall that the exchange of their rings was itself a statement of commitment, and so perhaps a small exchange of words blessing your rings and renewing that commitment might be significant. And, of course, always make a point of either visiting with or calling the people you love before you go and during your travels.

Every goodbye is potentially the last one: our lives are

fragile, and in acknowledging this we recognize that we owe our very breath to a higher being.

A parting prayer

The Lord watch between you and me when we are absent one from the other.

Genesis 31:49

4: WORK & STUDY

Wisdom is better than jewels, and all that you may desire cannot compare with her.

Proverbs 8:11

ESSAYS, PAPERS, AND PROJECTS

It always helps to start with an uncluttered work space. Bring something colourful to the space to encourage you, and always tidy up before leaving your work at the end of the day. It will help you concentrate on the importance of the project if you monitor progress each day or week. Use a graph or an outline picture or geometric design that is coloured in as you go. Incorporate some fun: one writer I know plays one game of solitaire on his computer at the start of each day. But be strict and don't end up playing the time away! Plot your progress each day or week. A visual representation works wonders. Try a pie chart to track your progress. When you finish, invite friends, family, or colleagues to mark the achievement. For yourself, consider the graph. What was good, or difficult? What have you learned, and what would you change another time? For a specially important project, make a collage of the remnants of notes, drawings or papers. Then throw all the old stuff out, clean your equipment and space ready for next project.

Exams

I will sound like your mother by saying there is no substitute for doing the work – but it's true! Once that is accomplished, though, chill out and relax. The night before the exam have a bath with restful oils, soothing music and candlelight. Having prepared well you can put the work to one side. Meditate in quietness, using something to help focus your thoughts, such as a picture or a stone. Pray. And once it's over, move on. Don't compare notes with others: they might be exaggerating what they did. Trust your instincts. Tidy your books away. Talk any anxieties through with someone you can trust and who can see the bigger picture. Then lay things to rest. Worrying will not improve your grades but might depress you.

First Interview

New clothes and a good hairstyle are good rituals for this: they really boost your morale. It's also a good idea to do some role play with someone who has been through it themselves. Hearing your own voice can be scary, especially if you find yourself stuttering, repeating things, or saying 'um' all the time. Always sort this out in advance. Think about how you will enter the room, what clothes you will wear (comfortable as well as appropriate). When the time arrives take three deep breaths before entering a room and walk with confidence. In advance, learn as much as you can about the job. Never say you can do things if you can't, but show willingness to learn new skills. Above all, be yourself: remember that scripture statement about people being 'made in the image of God' (Genesis 1:26–27). You truly are special: let that be seen.

Afterwards, assess your performance. What would you change another time? Review the position: would it really be a good fit for you? List pros and cons, and when you are offered the job sleep on it before making a decision. Discuss the implications of any changes that may affect other people in your life.

It is easy to become frustrated and lose confidence if you never get beyond the interview. Another person might be able to see things you have not appreciated, and help you assess your skills and present them well – either a professional agency or a friend. Practise in front of the mirror, and ask yourself whether you would give your reflection the job. If not, what would you change?

Working Away from Home

Business people travel a lot today, but no matter what the job, leaving family, friends, familiar scenes and cultural norms is always a challenge, even though there are many plus factors: new friends, the broadening of horizons, and new spiritual experiences. Technology has made a huge difference to the ways we deal with this, emails in particular. Many people find they can nurture relationships through email and communicate things that would be hard to say face to face. Let this work for you: as you give, you will discover you receive much more in return, and old relationships can take off in new directions through this medium. But as well as keeping in touch with home, explore the soul of your temporary location. Visit the museums, and listen to the poets, storytellers and artists, who are frequently the most spiritually articulate people in any culture.

Sabbatical

The term sabbatical derives from the Sabbath, the seventh and final day in the ancient Hebrew story of creation on which God rested.[4] Humankind appears on the sixth day, which means the first priority in the life of people was to rest! In a 24/7 world, we need to rediscover this, and growing numbers of people now take a sabbatical from work. In countries like Australia and New Zealand 'long service leave' is a regular provision in employment contracts – either as a period for research or writing, or just a chance to recharge one's batteries. If it is possible to go to another place, be intentional in searching out a new ritual from the people you meet, especially if you are fortunate enough to visit another culture than your own. It is easy to dissipate the time and not accomplish the goals you have set for yourself, so build in specific opportunities to try some new skill and make something creative. In particular, try something you would not attempt at home. Search out the spirituality of the place you are in: you may find that other cultures have a tradition you could adopt for yourself that would enhance your own life and those you care for.

RESIGNING FROM WORK

Submitting your formal notice will be the easy bit. On a personal level, resigning from a position can be potentially distressing. If you are leaving because of some disagreement, take time to reflect on whether this is what you definitely want to do rather than responding to the heat of the moment. In any event, you want to leave amicably and with decorum, so avoid confrontation – though if you are leaving because of unpleasant working conditions there is no need for you to pretend otherwise. You can be agreeable while still being truthful. Visualize in advance how you want the conversation to go, see yourself keeping calm and in control of the situation. You are a person of value and worth, so no one should take advantage of you. If they try to do so, by not stooping to their level of behaviour you will deny them the advantage. In working through tricky situations, make a collage, take symbols from magazines, papers, maybe even work brochures and use them as a way of exorcising the past. Burn it if it is something to be forgotten, frame it if it has been a liberating experience. Maybe take a special bath and allow the water to cleanse you ready for a new start.

Losing your Job

There are invariably financial implications in losing your job, though it is often the emotional challenge that causes most problems. We can generally live on less money, but it is a devastating thing to lose a sense of identity, and for people in Western culture work is a major source of meaning and purpose. It may not be easy to see new opportunities in this hardship, but it can be done. The balance sheet can be a useful tool,[5] and including things that have no obvious monetary value can offer a different perspective on life. Journal, graphs, meditation and visualization are other helpful resources. Sound financial advice will help, and we should also address personal matters. The support of others is essential. Take a realistic look at what you have achieved, because no one is ever a total failure. If you lose your job along with other colleagues, then stick together: the benefit of being in community and linked to others with the same struggle will be enormous. For those with no immediate prospects of new employment, there are plenty of organizations that will use your skills, even though they may not be able to pay more than expenses. You may even discover skills you never thought you had that can be an asset for your future. Determine clear aims and objectives for your future – but always be realistic about what is possible so as not to set yourself up for predictable failure.

A New Job

When my daughter-in-law started a new job, I sent her two yucca plants to fill some of the space in her rather large office and to be a daily reminder that I was thinking of her. They flourished, and so did she. But after some time she decided to move on because things were not working out. She left as a matter of integrity to herself without knowing where the next job would come from, and took the plants home. One was sick and one had died. This spoke to her of work-life balance. She felt the dead one should go – part of the old experience – and the sick one she lovingly tended and watered over the next weeks while she had no work. Then two new shoots started to sprout. Hope was springing, and today she has her own thriving creative business. She told me that caring for this plant became a significant ritual – and it is now blooming in the new office.

I called my son to see if he was ready to start his new job. 'Yes', he said, 'I've done a dry run.' He had made himself a spreadsheet of the times of buses, costs, and so on, and had worked out where to wait for the train and how long it would all take so he would arrive there in time. This was the beginning of a new routine, and figuring things out in advance can be a good ritual to minimize the anxiety of a new situation. Even if you don't have transportation to organize, you will need to gather appropriate equipment and get your uniform or new clothes. A graph, journal or scrap-book is especially useful at the start while you adjust to your new conditions. Record small achievements and every detail of progress. Give yourself time to settle. Perhaps find a relevant word of wisdom and put it up at home or work to encourage you.

5: Facing ourselves

People are changed not by ethical urgings, but by transformed imagination

Paul Ricoeur, French philosopher (1913–2005)

Discovering the Big Picture

I distinctly recall the occasion when as a teenager I became aware of how unjust life can be. I sometimes wish the passion with which I felt it then was still with me, though the feeling has never quite gone. I would not wish to eradicate this sense of injustice, though simply being angry is not enough: we need to learn to channel our energy in ways that can facilitate change. Things can seem deceptively simple when we are young, and the secret is how to become better informed while not losing our cutting edge in terms of honesty, integrity and a willingness to help bring about change. The ritual here may be to commit to doing something, perhaps by joining a pressure group that will offer creative solutions, but will also enable us in the process to see the bigger picture. Or you could do something much simpler. Consider the route you travel to work. Do you pass waste land? Why not scatter some hardy annual seeds such as poppies or marigolds. Take a bottle of water to encourage their germination, and as you pass look out for signs of growth, recognizing the possibility of transformation in all of life. Knowing that you have been part of this small change for the better, reflect on how you might be part of a bigger picture. It takes time for seeds to grow, and it takes time for ideas to come to fruition. Discover the value of patient reflection as distinct from intemperate – and potentially damaging – instinctive reaction.

FEAR

Fear is an underlying theme in many of the topics mentioned in this chapter. It takes many forms, and can be devastating when it grips us – whether it is an apparently simple fear such as going to the dentist, or the communal paranoia induced by the threat of terrorist activity in our midst. We all respond differently, and what is insignificant to one person seems like an insurmountable mountain to another. Fears can be addressed by facing them. We often imagine every possible scenario, when the reality is that only one outcome is likely. That recognition can itself be hugely reassuring, and a simple reminder of it can become a ritual. Expressing our anxieties in a journal can also be a useful way of identifying for ourselves what triggers them. Some people use commercial relaxation tapes as part of the process, while others put words to music themselves, either composing their own words or using ready-made ones, such as the wisdom literature of the Hebrew scriptures (Psalms, Job, Proverbs, Ecclesiastes). Creating movements to accompany the words and music can also be helpful. When we identify a ritual that helps then we should be intentional in using it. Like physical exercise, such things are more effective with practice.

The immediacy with which violence of all kinds is reported today is creating a widespread sense of fearfulness in our culture. We now see war and terrorist incidents on the television screen unedited, and frequently without any wider context. It is inevitable that we all get caught up in the drama of the moment, though the intensity with which we are affected depends on how near the centre of the disaster we live or if we have a particular friend or loved one caught up in the tragedy. Some people have become addicted to watching dramatic tragedies as they unfold on the various news channels. In order to break this cycle some people (particularly those with a relative involved in recent armed struggles) have found practical rituals through use of their computers, not only sharing accurate information through dedicated websites but also offering support to others in a similar position through emails and blogging.

Fear is that little darkroom where
negatives are developed
> *Michael Pritchard, American TV presenter*

Temptation

It is often not possible to remove a temptation so you may have to remove yourself – whether the problem is over-eating (don't go where the food is) or an unhealthy relationship (sever contact with the person involved). Get a friend to support you, break the problem down into things to be tackled each day, and use a graph or diary to chart your progress. Note if some particular things cause you to lose control: if you identify specific triggers you are well placed to take action.

BEING LATE FOR THINGS

If this is habitual then you need to take a look at why you are late. Do you take too many things on, try to do too many things in too short a time, or do you fritter away time? It is discourteous to be late regularly, so establish the reasons, list them and work out what changes you can make. Plan to set off for appointments ten minutes earlier than you need to. Put your watch or clock ten minutes fast. If that still doesn't work, move the clock twenty minutes forward!

CAUSING SOMETHING TO GO WRONG

It might be just a slip of the tongue, or neglecting to pass on vital information at work, or losing concentration while driving and creating a hazardous outcome. Simple actions can have devastating consequences, and knowing that we were responsible can weigh heavily on the mind for a very long time. Another person can assist in getting the situation in perspective, though it is not helpful when others try to suggest that we were not to blame. If the mistake was ours, we rarely find peace by ignoring it. When we accept responsibility, the consequences are not always as bad as we imagine they might be, and quite often the liability will rest with more than one person. Working through this is likely to be tough, so be in a place of some significance to you. Decide whether to be alone or with others. Water has traditionally been used in rituals of cleansing and forgiveness. Perhaps wash your hands or have them washed for you. You may wish to ask for prayer: this will be essential to your well-being and knowledge of forgiveness if you believe yourself to have offended a higher being. Think especially carefully about whether it would be appropriate to involve the person you have wronged. Take advice, and plenty of time. Perhaps write down an account of what went wrong and how you feel. You might want to burn the papers to ash, and then use the ash to make a sign or a message on paper – something that could be framed to remind you of your decision, or copied and sent to significant people. There is no point in doing this kind of thing just to cause a fuss and draw attention to yourself: you need to be committed to change, otherwise such rituals can actually become unhelpful. Have someone say words of healing over you and anoint you with oil on hands, feet, or forehead, to acknowledge your decision and encourage you to go forward. Perhaps invite them to call you and have a drink on the anniversary of this event to see how you are progressing. It could become an annual ritual.

BAD EXPERIENCES

A lot depends on the severity of the experience. Refuse to let these things rule your life, and design a ritual that allows you to lay them to rest. Sometimes, writing and shredding or burning is effective. Doing hard physical work is also a good ritual, especially if it does not demand great concentration, because this allows you to sort out the jumble of thoughts in your head. What happens when you have been to an event which turned out to be bad when you expected something different – a movie, a sports event, a church service? Reflect on your feelings. Is there anything of value to be retrieved? What would have made it better? How would you have changed it had you been responsible? Would other people have had difficulty with your changes? Is there anything practical you might do that could have a positive outcome? Writing to a representative? Organizing a petition? Is there political action you could be part of?

GETTING PLACED SECOND

Coming first is exciting – you've made it. Coming third is good: you could have been fourth and missed being placed! But coming second can be especially disappointing because you have just missed out on first place. Acknowledge your achievement: if you know you gave it your best shot, enjoy your success. If you think you could have done better, talk it through with your coach or mentor for a truthful assessment as well as support. Set your future goals and plan how to improve. Be generous in congratulating the person who was first, and encourage the one who came third. Don't take your disappointment out on folk who have helped you to get where you are: if you do that you are in danger of becoming a real loser, despite your success. Incorporate these attitudes into lifestyle: it will actually transform who you are becoming, which is ultimately more important than simply winning. Value your progress by keeping a record of your achievements: press cuttings, family photos, programmes, and so on. Preserve them in a quality binder or attractively decorated scrap book: its actual appearance will say something about your worth. Look back over it and see just how far you have come. My eldest son took to cross-country running in high school. He enjoyed the challenge and trained hard, and on one occasion surprised everyone – including himself – by coming ninth in the Scottish Championships. But at the school's annual sports day he invariably came second. I used to say, 'Well, if you just tried a little bit harder you'd get a chance at being first.' It was only some years later that we all realized he'd really given it his very best shot, as the boy who regularly ran faster went on to run internationally for his country! Know the competition, as well as yourself – and don't let others be too hard on you.

Depression

Feeling miserable is not necessarily the same thing as being depressed. Clinical depression requires medical help in the same way as any other health condition would, so if you are continually feeling down see the doctor to establish whether there is a physiological explanation. If you are just fed up then making a graph over a period of time can provide a visual picture of your mood swings and show if there is a regular pattern. Some obvious reasons may emerge from this, in which case you need to take steps to change misery-inducing situations. If a particular individual has a negative effect on you, then spend less time with them. Create change, whether it is the physical space, the routine, the order you do things, the way you do things, your diet, or whatever. Just doing this can create a feeling of renewed well-being. Then give yourself some treats – buy yourself some flowers, pamper yourself with a relaxing bathtime ritual, look up old acquaintances, take up some new activity that you enjoy – and above all, have some fun.

Saying Sorry

When you've messed up there is no short cut to apologizing. We have to mean it, and if we are sincere that should help us to avoid doing the same thing again. We all have rituals for saying sorry. But a rushed apology can be as bad as no apology. This requires quality time and appropriate symbols. A single flower can on occasion convey a more significant message than a lavish bouquet. Remember what I suggested at the very beginning of this book, that the usefulness of a ritual depends on the meaning that is invested in it.

At the same time, we should never confuse confront-ational argument with a good provocative dialogue. Learning to engage with different points of view without aggression is an important life skill. We need to see the other person's point of view, and present our own feelings calmly. Sometimes we end up fighting because we cannot put our feelings into words. Even if that is not your style, still take a good look at how you behave in such situations. It is also possible to remain calm yet still aggressive by goading another person to back themselves into a corner from which escape will be difficult. Well-educated people often have highly developed oral skills, and can enjoy watching others get angry, maybe even deliberately provoking them in some way. If you are aware of this in yourself, be intentional in your desire to change and seek out help.

So how can we end an argument and live in peace and with tolerance for others? One ritual would be to exchange specific tokens: friendship bracelets could be especially useful in this context because they take time to make, allowing space to reflect on why we spoke out of turn and how we can prevent this in the future. These are strips of coloured thread, cord or leather woven together. If you create a stock of them in advance it may help you to pause before entering into an argument in the first place. If you collect too many of them, maybe it's time to ask why you are fighting so much. Are you under pressure or feeling threatened in some way? Can you prevent it? If you argue repeatedly with the same person you could make a ritual of exchanging the same bracelet every time. It might enable you to laugh at your folly and slow you down in future. You could try cleaning opposite sides of the same window, or if you are still having difficulty why not try wearing a red nose each? Adults can be a bit too self-opinionated to do this kind of fun thing, but children love it. Of course, they are often more ready to forgive in the first place.

Prevention is always better than cure, and a moment's pause for thought can avoid an unnecessary explosion of rage. Don't confuse this with just suppressing anger: some people do that so regularly they no longer have the ability to confront issues in helpful ways (a tactic that appeals to some personality types and is also encouraged by certain cultures). In the early days of their relationship, a couple I know would make a visit to the glass recycling bank whenever they needed to offload their anger. As they smashed the bottles into the containers, they would name the problematic situations or individuals, with the only rule being that they could not name each other in this way.

WHEN GOD SEEMS FAR AWAY

To start with, tell God – who is even more interested than you are in coming near. Tell a friend you can trust to pray for you when you do not feel you can pray for yourself. At this point many people find the work of artists speaks into their situation in a way that words cannot address, so take the opportunity to visit any galleries near to you.

WHEN THE WORLD IS A LONELY PLACE

Be intentional in finding some new friends. Join some events or classes where you will be doing things you enjoy, and the friends will come as a by-product. Offer yourself to some voluntary organizations: working for others is a great way of diverting your attention away from yourself. And remember that word of ancient wisdom: 'Those who would have friends must first show themselves to be friendly.'[6]

Chapter 1: Rituals and Reflections

1. On these events and their significance, see John Drane, *Cultural Change and Biblical Faith* (Carlisle: Paternoster Press 2000), 78–103.
2. Mary Douglas, *Natural Symbols* (New York: Random House 1973), 20.
3. Leonel L. Mitchell, *The Meaning of Ritual* (New York: Paulist 1977).
4. Robert Fulghum, *From Beginning to End: the rituals of our lives* (New York: Ivy Books 1995).
5. Tom F. Driver, *The Magic of Ritual* (New York: HarperCollins 1991), 3.
6. John M. Lundquist, *The Temple: meeting place of heaven and earth* (London: Thames & Hudson 1993), 20.
7. Leonel Mitchell, *The Meaning of Ritual*, 117.
8. Nicholas Wolterstorff, *Lament for a Son* (London: SPCK 1997); Olive M. Fleming Drane, *Clowns, Storytellers, Disciples* (Oxford: BRF 2000).
9. Psalm 8:3–9.

Chapter 2: Beginnings and Endings

1. See http://www.frankwater.com
2. Proverbs 3:5, 6
3. James 1:5, 6
4. For more on this, see chapter 1.
5. For a description of this, see chapter 1.
6. For an example, see http://nat.uca.org.au/TD/worship/Orders_of_Service/heal_end_mar.htm (the website of the Uniting Church in Australia).
7. For more on this, see www.christianvocations.org
8. John 12:24.
9. John 11:25.

Chapter 3: Times and Seasons

1. Deuteronomy 6:4–9, 'Hear O Israel: Keep these words ... write them on the doorposts of your house and on your gates.'
2. On creating a journal, see chapter 1.
3. For more on this, see chapter 1.
4. On signatures, see chapter 1.
5. For more on this, see chapter 2.
6. For this, see John Drane and Olive M. Fleming Drane, *Family Fortunes: Faith-full caring for today's families* (London: Darton Longman & Todd 2004), 118–141.
7. David Hay, *The Spirit of the Child* (London: Fount 1998).
8. Genesis 1:31.
9. Psalm 139:13.
10. Eric H. Erikson, *Identity and the life cycle; selected papers, with a historical introd. by David Rapaport* (New York: International Universities Press 1959).
11. For ideas on how to do this, see Mike Paterson, *With Love: gifting stories to grandchildren* (North Shore City, New Zealand: Tandem Press 2001, 2nd edn).
12. For more on keeping a journal, see chapter 1.

Chapter 4: Everyday Life

1. For further information on traditional Jewish practices today, see Alfred J. Kolatch, *The Jewish Home Advisor* (New York: Jonathan David Publishers 1990).
2. For some ideas, see http://www.beliefnet.com, http://www.ship-of-fools. com, http://www.clubberstemple.com, http://www.religion-online. org, http://www.shootthemessenger.com.au, http://www.hollywoodjesus.com, http://www.godweb.org, http://www.rejesus.co.uk, http://onearthasin heaven.co.uk, http://theooze.com; for a weekly spiritual comment on a current issue, visit http://www.licc.org.uk and ask to be put on their mailing list; and for an online labyrinth, http://www.yfc.co.uk/labyrinth/online.html
3. For this, see chapter 2.
4. For more elaborate instructions, see http://www.nativetech.org/dreamcat/dreminst.html
5. Ian M. Fraser, *Reinventing Church: insights from small Christian communities and reflections on a journey among them* (privately published by the author, no date, but early 1990s).
6. Deuteronomy 6:5.